MOTORCYCLE ADVENTURER

MOTORCYCLE ADVENTURER

CARL STEARNS CLANCY: FIRST MOTORCYCLIST TO RIDE AROUND THE WORLD 1912-1913

DR. GREGORY W. FRAZIER

iUniverse, Inc.
New York Bloomington

MOTORCYCLE ADVENTURER
Carl Stearns Clancy: First Motorcyclist To Ride Around The World 1912-1913

iUniverse books may be ordered through booksellers or by contacting:

iUniverse
1663 Liberty Drive
Bloomington, IN 47403
www.iuniverse.com
1-800-Authors (1-800-288-4677)

Because of the dynamic nature of the Internet, any Web addresses or links contained in this book may have changed since publication and may no longer be valid. The views expressed in this work are solely those of the author and do not necessarily reflect the views of the publisher, and the publisher hereby disclaims any responsibility for them.

ISBN: 978-1-4502-2141-2 (sc)
ISBN: 978-1-4502-2140-5 (ebk)

Printed in the United States of America

iUniverse rev. date: 04/02/2010

TABLE OF CONTENTS

PREFACE

D anger, guns, unfriendly natives, and the largest and "world's fastest" motorcycle were just four of the multitude of risky elements that made up the first circumnavigation of the globe by a motorcyclist.

The Search for the Clancy Story

I am blessed with the ownership of a Henderson motorcycle. In 1994, Richard Henry Schultz published a Limited Collector's Edition of his book, *Hendersons, those Elegant Machines, the Complete History of Henderson Motorcycles (1911-1931)*. Being one of the enthusiastic owners of a Henderson, I purchased his book.

While fondling and reading the coffee table book, I found a small three-sentence paragraph about Carl Stearns Clancy and his accomplishment of riding a 1912 Henderson around the world in 1912 and 1913. Schultz had also included in his book a full-page copy from a 1913 sales brochure from the Henderson Company of Clancy sitting on his motorcycle after completing his ride around the globe. I was hooked like a starving fish, wanting to learn more about this monumental feat.

A telephone call to Schultz found him to be gracious and anxious to talk about Henderson motorcycles to a fellow enthusiast. When I asked about Clancy, the picture in his book, and what he knew of the first motorcycle ride about the world, Schultz said only that he had come across some references and the sales brochure in the original Henderson files while researching the company. I began to back track his research, trying to find a thread to his source documents, then the originals. The search took me into numerous dusty archives of museums, libraries and following a number of false leads from word-of-mouth sources in the Henderson and motorcycle community.

As I began to learn more about Clancy I found we had much in common, albeit many years apart. He and I had covered much of the same ground, so when he was writing about distant places like Japan, Africa or Europe I could relate to what he had seen and some of the cultures he was passing through. Again, like Clancy, I would return to some of those places with movie cameras while we traveled to pay our way. And, like Clancy, we both wrote books. I smiled when I discovered Clancy had written a film titled *The Adventurous Sex*, remembering when I had written an early book titled *Motorcycle Sex*. Finally, both Clancy and I were loyal to our Henderson motorcycles.

One of the questions that kept me hunting was Clancy's riding attire. In many of the photographs, he was shown wearing a coat, white shirt and tie, a very classy act for a hardened and road weary traveler. It still strikes me as a serious commitment to present a positive image of motorcycling to carry in his limited luggage a dress suit for these photographic and media opportunities.

At the American Motorcycle Hall of Fame Museum I discovered several aged and out-of-sequence copies of the articles written by Clancy and published in a bicycle and motorcycle magazine, *The Bicycling World and Motorcycle Review*. One installment indicated that Clancy had not started out alone but was accompanied by Walter Storey, also riding a 1912 Henderson. The faded photocopies were in mixed boxes with the original design drawings of Henderson motorcycles, agreements between the Henderson owners and eventual buyer, and numerous accounting records. Once I had these few photocopies I had a solid thread to follow to find the entire story of the Clancy adventure.

The Magazine

The Bicycling World and Motorcycle Review was a weekly publication based in the city of New York. The first of 24 installments by Clancy was published on November 26, 1912. The final Clancy installment was published on February 3, 1914.

The last issue of the magazine itself was dated February 2, 1915, after which it was absorbed by another motorcycle magazine, *Motorcycle Illustrated*, the magazine which published what was included and titled herein as the Epilogue. My hunt for each company's archives came up empty. However, some missing copies were found at antique motorcycle flea markets and in the bowels of public libraries.

The Adventure

Thousands of motorcycle riders, some solo, others with pillions, an occasional sidecar and motorized trike driver, ranging from 50cc to 2000cc, have been circumnavigating the globe for nearly 100 years. Many of the pilots and owners feel their accomplishment was a first or enlightened in some way. Most have never heard of Carl Stearns Clancy, an equal number likely not knowing of a Henderson motorcycle.

As I researched the Clancy adventure there surfaced several pivotal points where the accomplishment of being the first person

DR. GREGORY W. FRAZIER

to circumnavigate the globe on a motorcycle might never have happened.

The first was deciding to make the attempt, something for which both Clancy and Storey deserve credit. The second was being able to put together the financial resources to pay for the adventure. Securing Henderson Company backing and obviously the magazine paying for articles required a strong sales pitch, again something for which I believe both Storey and Clancy deserve credit.

Clancy deciding to go onward alone after Storey had to abandon his side of the trip was a major turning point. This was no easy decision on the part of Clancy, because the ground he and Storey had covered to that point was a known, albeit tough, road. Leaving Europe for the vast unknown of Africa, alone, reflected a man with dedication and a real spirit of adventure.

Clancy's flexibility when faced with trip-ending barriers, like no roads, outrageous expenses and bureaucratic hassles, again reflected a man willing to take risks, manage them, adjust and move forward. One of the words in the definition of adventure is risk. Clancy faced and managed real motorcycling risks.

The tedium of typing on his portable typewriter the words that were then mailed off to New York was far removed from what modern-day adventurers face with electronic gizmos to post on the Internet their words and pictures, within hours of shutting off their motorcycles. I have pictured the stress Clancy must have had to face in cramped ship quarters typing. Or the hassles associated with trying to get roll film developed for pictures to be sent along with his words to his publisher.

In an article titled, "Motorcycles Set New Marks for Power and Reliability in 1913," published in the *The Syracuse Herald* newspaper, January 27, 1914, Clancy was quoted as saying about travel by motorcycle: "…for anyone who desires to diverge from the beaten path and visit points that may be of peculiar interest to him personally, the motorcycle is undoubtedly the only satisfactory means of travel."

The 1912 Henderson Motorcycle

Four cylinders, no front brake, one gear, and a unique hand-crank starter were part of what made the "fastest motorcycle in the world" in 1912. With 7 horsepower and a 57 cubic inch (934cc) engine, it was first available in January, 1912, and sold for $325.00. The lever on the left side of the gas tank was not a shift lever, but an "eclipse" clutch-engage lever to let the engine power transfer to the rear wheel or not. The gas tank held three gallons of gas and in a separate compartment two quarts of oil. The motorcycle was long, with a 65-inch wheelbase. It had an external rear band brake operated by the right or left foot above the floorboard in front of the driver.

For carrying a passenger, there was an optional seat that attached to the frame in front of the driver. The passenger would stabilize himself by placing his feet on slight extensions to the front axle and holding onto the crossover on the handlebars.

The Henderson Motorcycle Company was founded in 1911 and initially located at 268 Jefferson Avenue, in Detroit, Michigan. The company was formed by two brothers, William G. Henderson and Thomas Henderson, Jr. Their father and Thomas Jr. had both worked for a car company earlier, the Winton Motor Car Company. There they got a taste of record-setting, when Dr. Horatio Nelson Jackson became the first person to drive an automobile (a Winton) across the United States, from San Francisco, California, to New York City. Ten years later, when

Thomas Jr. and William were approached by adventurists Clancy and Storey, the Henderson brothers were well aware of the positive marketing impact a record-setting motorcycle ride around the globe could have for the new company if the motorcyclists used their 1912 model.

The company was sold in 1917, to Ignaz Schwinn, the manufacturer of Schwinn bicycles and Excelsior Motorcycles.

Carl Stearns Clancy

Born August 8, 1890, in Epping, New Hampshire, Carl Stearns Clancy was 22 years old when he started his journey around the globe with Walter Storey on October 5, 1912. Clancy died in January, 1971, in Alexandria, Virginia, having lived a full and adventurous life over his 80-plus years.

While this book was not intended to be a biography of Clancy's life, during fact and back checking some interesting accomplishments of note surfaced that pointed to his life as a traveler, writer, film producer and director, but most of all an adventurer:

- The 1900 Federal Census listed his age as 9 and living in Brimfield, Massachusetts, with his mother Alice E. Clancy (age 52), father William P. Clancy (age 55). His father's birthplace was noted as Ireland, while his mother was born in Massachusetts. William P. Clancy's occupation was described as Clergyman.

- The 1910 Federal Census listed Clancy as living in Canton, Massachusetts, still single.

- Marriage Records from Santa Clara County, California, recorded Carl Stearns Clancy marrying on April 8, 1916.

- The World War I Draft Registration Card Clancy filled out on June 5, 1917, listed his occupation as Publicity Writer, living at 1711 Vine Street in Hollywood, California, age 26.

- The 1920 Federal Census listed Clancy, at the age of 29, as being married, living in New York City, and his occupation being an Author in the Motion Picture industry.

- In 1922, Clancy was the writer and producer of a film titled *The Headless Horseman* (an adaptation starring Will Rogers).

- On October 23, 1922, Clancy was shown as arriving at Plymouth, England, on the ship *France*, having departed from New York and listing his occupation as Motion Picture Producer, age 32.

- On February 9, 1923, Clancy arrived back in the United States on the ship *Patria*, having departed from Naples, Italy, on January 26, 1923.

- 1923 was the year Clancy wrote an adaptation for the film *Six Cylinder Love*.

- In 1925, Clancy was the writer for a silent film titled *The Adventurous Sex*.

- In 1926, Clancy was the producer for a film titled *Churchyards of Old America*.

- On September 27, 1926, Clancy was shown as a passenger arriving on the ship *Leviathan* in New York, having departed Cherbourg, France, on September 21, his age being 36, and having an address on Wall Street, New York City.

- In 1927, a book by Clancy was published titled *The Viking Ship*.

- Between 1927 and the end of 1928, Clancy produced and directed 12 films starring Will Rogers, with the following titles: *With Will Rogers in Dublin, Hiking Through Holland with Will Rogers, With Will Rogers in Paris, Hunting for Germans in Berlin with Will Rogers, Through Switzerland and Bavaria with will Rogers, With Will Rogers in London, Roaming the Emerald Isle with Will Rogers, Prowling Around France with Will Rogers, Winging Around Europe with Will Rogers, Exploring England with Will Rogers, Reeling Down the Rhine with Will Rogers,* and *Over the Bounding Blue with Will Rogers.*

- On September 10, 1928, Clancy was shown as arriving in New York City from Oslo, Norway, on the ship *Stavangerfjord*, age 38, and having an address in New York City.

- The 1930 Federal Census listed Clancy, age 39, living in Los Angeles, California.

- On July 24, 1932, the Passenger List for the ship *De Grasse*, having departed Havre, France, shows Clancy arriving in New York, age 42, with an address of Port Washington, New York. He was accompanied by his second wife.

- On July 15, 1935, Clancy, age 45, was listed as arriving from New York on the ship *Europa*, at Southhampton, England, with a New York City residence address.

- On November 18, 1936, Clancy made a 12-day roundtrip trip from New York and back on the ship *Haiti*, showing his age as 46 and the same address as before in New York City.

- On March 18, 1938, Clancy was listed on the Passenger List for the ship *Exochorda*, arriving in New York from Mediterranean Ports, age 47, and accompanied by his wife, both listing the same previous address in New York City as their residence.

- Clancy's U.S. World War II Draft Registration card completed on April 27, 1942, listed his age as 51, and living in Alexandria, Virginia, working for the U.S. Forest Service, Washington, D.C.

- 1948 government records announced a film released theatrically through the U.S. Department of Agriculture, Forest Service, directed by Carl Stearns Clancy. Its running time was 7.32 minutes, was in color, and had cartoon characters, the main ones being Junior Raindrop and Father Cloud. A synopsis described the film as being about a delinquent raindrop explaining the need for good watershed management. The title of the film: *The Adventures of Junior Raindrop*.

- In 1956, a second book by Clancy was published, titled, *The Saga of Leif Ericsson, Discoverer of America*.

Walter Rendell Storey

Walter Rendell Storey was born in Philadelphia, Pennsylvania, on June 22, 1881. He had a twin brother named Charles with whom he lived when the 1910 census was taken. At the time of the start of the first attempted motorcycle ride around the world, Walter Storey was living in the city of New York. The 1910 census form indicated his father and mother were from England, that he was single at the time, and his job was with the Board of Motion Pictures.

Storey was 31 years old when he started out with Carl Stearns Clancy on their attempt to circle the globe. On his passport application, dated the 25th day of September, 1912, he listed his occupation as Secretary. However, on the passenger list for the ship he left on from Philadelphia with Clancy, the *Merion*, which arrived in Liverpool on October 17, 1912, his Occupation or Profession was listed as Advertiser. A possible explanation was whoever prepared the manifest reversed the Clancy and Storey Occupations as Storey was listed above Clancy on the one-page form, Clancy's Occupation being listed as Secretary. On his WWII draft registration, Storey hand-wrote that he worked for *The New York Times*, was 60 years old, married to Helen A. Storey, and both were living in Bergen, New Jersey.

This Book

Carl Stearns Clancy was quoted in an announcement published in the magazine, *The Bicycling World and Motorcycle Review*, saying that he and Mr. Storey would attempt to make the first motorcycle ride around the world, and "As we must pay part of our expenses by writing articles for American and foreign magazines and newspapers enroute, and by publishing a complete book upon our return..." For unknown reasons, the referenced book was never published.

Once I had a major portion of the actual published installments, I began back checking some of the details to ensure what was fact and not fiction. This included looking at many small details, then comparing them to sections in the installments. For instance, a review of the *California Passenger and Crew Lists, 1893-1957*, showed that Carl S. Clancy was listed as arriving in San Francisco, California, May 13, 1913, on the ship *Star of Persia*, departing from Hong Kong, China. A note in the 2nd class Passenger section showed that Clancy boarded in Yokohama. This confirmed his narrative in Chapter XIX, published September 2, 1913.

When I began trying to find a publishing company to move this book into print, all known motorcycle book publishers contacted turned the project down. Reasons ranged from "budgetary cuts" to "We're over-committed now." Other reasons included, "The Henderson Motorcycle Company has died, twice, so there will be little interest in these motorcycles other than to few Henderson collectors" and "It won't sell, there was no sex, drugs and rock 'n roll on his adventure, that's what we need to sell books."

When Arrowstar Publishing provided a way to publish the mass of material collected, some decisions had to be made in formatting, layout, and design. This editorial process led to choosing to publish the text of the Clancy installments as they were printed in the magazine, including obvious errors. We felt Clancy, in his writing from the road, may have intentionally used words in a certain way, spelled them as they were spelled at the time or knowingly made a transposition. The same decision was made with the obvious printed errors in the magazine. For instance, in the Prologue, the caption under a photograph of Clancy had his name misspelled. Rather than our editors correcting it, we left it as it was published, as we did other errors, to give the reader of this book a taste for the way the original words were presented.

Pictures in this book required that we take some liberties in their placement. Sometimes a picture was placed by the magazine editors well away from the text which referenced it. Once we found an obvious photograph taken by Clancy that was included in the text of another article in the magazine. In that case, we placed the picture in the Clancy text where we felt it made the most sense, where Clancy was referring to the content of the photograph. With the placement of the photographs we were trying to maintain the integrity of the Clancy text while incorporating images his editors in New York were making decisions on to meet space requirements.

The photographs were old, and of poor quality, but we opted to use what we had and not use computer enhancements to improve them. We did cut some photographs away from adjoining photographs to enable us to place them in the Clancy text where they could stand on their own.

While finishing some of the research on the book I asked double Guinness World Record holder and American Motorcycle Hall of Fame member Dave Barr to write the Introduction. I had discussed the project with Barr several times up to that point, so he knew numerous facts about the content of the book. What I asked him to do in the Introduction was to try to imagine what Clancy was facing in 1912 and 1913 while he worked his way around the world. Barr had successfully completed a three and one-half year, 83,000 mile ride around the world on a 1972 Harley-Davidson under very arduous conditions, including two prosthetic legs. His book *Riding the Edge* recounts his amazing adventure.

Similar to Clancy's ride around the world, this book has made many stops and re-starts. And as with Clancy, I was faced with decisions to push forward or abandon the effort. If you are reading this book you know I decided, like Clancy, to go forward with the project. Carl Stearns Clancy made the first motorcycle ride around the world and I was intent on helping him complete his book about this incredible accomplishment.

ACKNOWLEDGMENTS

Like Carl Stearns Clancy's ride around the world, this book took many twists and turns over a 16-year period towards completion with the help of many avid motorcyclists, historians and researchers along the way.

Richard Henry Schultz, who wrote in his 1994 book, *Hendersons, Those Elegant Machines, The Complete History of Henderson Motorcycles (1911-1931)*, a limited collector's edition, provided the initial spark for this publication with a small three-sentence paragraph reference to Clancy's accomplishment and copy of Clancy on his 1912 Henderson from a Henderson company sales brochure in his 1994 book. The last sentence read, "This feat must have had an impact on the motorcycling world."

Andy Goldfine, "Mr. Aerostich" of the Aerostich/RiderWearHouse Company, convinced me to undertake the final form for this book project. An avid adventurer and motorcycle intellectual, Goldfine repeatedly encouraged me to continue with my research for the sake of the recording the historical significance of Clancy's incredible accomplishment.

Dave Barr, a double Guinness World Record holder for his adventure motorcycling accomplishments and member of the American Motorcycle Hall of Fame, greatly helped by filling in some of what I thought to be were serious holes in the Clancy tale.

Jean Fairclough, researcher extraordinaire and manuscript manager rooted out some of the previously unknown details of the history of Clancy. Her persistence pushed me towards completion after the book project was tossed on the rocks by unsupportive publishers.

Richard Livermore was responsible for most of the photographs and a major portion of the text making it into the final treatment. A motorcycle enthusiast and Honda CX650 collector, he did what I could not in the bowels of the dusty achieves of a library, pushing the project forward when the time and necessary financial resources needed for continued research were about to bring the project to a halt.

Stanley B. Myers, successful BMW and Indian motorcycle racer, mechanical guru and my adopted father needs special thanks for helping me acquire much of my motorcycle and mechanical knowledge, numerous go-fast riding and survival tips and tricks and most importantly, in the context of this publication, my Henderson motorcycle.

I am indebted to several museums, libraries and their personnel for immeasurable assistance. The American Motorcycle Hall of Fame Museum, Museum of Science and Industry, and The Bicycle Museum of America provided research material and direction. The New York Public Library, Public Library of Cincinnati and Hamilton County, Chicago Public Library, Detroit Public Library and Smithsonian Library all played a role in the assemblage of the final collection of magazine publications.

Two individuals, unbeknownst to them, played major roles towards the completion of the *Motorcycle Adventurer* project. Mark Mederski gave me professional advice and direction when my research had stalled. George Snyder, an author of over 28 books and numerous stories and articles, encouraged me to ignore the advice of well-established publishing houses and their representatives to shelve the project. Snyder nearly parroted Clancy when Clancy wrote about what others told him during his ride around the world. The Clancy mottos about what was up ahead were, "Never believe what you hear," and "Take nothing for granted."

Arrowstar Publishing and the Whole Earth Motorcycle Center provided the direction and "glue" to bring the numerous threads, published articles and pictures together in the final form of a book and supplemental CD (www.motorcycleadventurer.com).

James W. Aiken, fellow motorcycle pilot and gifted lawyer, made considerable contributions along the way, too numerous to detail.

Legal inspiration came via Marilyn McRae giving direction and counsel needed to sort through some litigious bumps in the road.

Finally, William Henderson and his brother Tom Henderson Jr. have to be acknowledged for their faith, commitment and support for the first circumnavigation of the globe on a motorcycle. Their company was started in 1911 and somehow Clancy and Storey convinced the Henderson brothers to support the incredible attempt to be the first to "girdle the globe" by motorcycle. Common to all motorcyclists dreaming of riding around the world, these entrepreneurial brothers combined their dreams with financial reality for there to be a first motorcycle ride around the world.

INTRODUCTION
By Dave Barr

This man Clancy was every bit a true adventurer. He struck out on more than an "adventure of a lifetime," it was an adventure none of us could do today, so it was more like a motorcycle adventure of the century. To ride off into the unknown, where there were no maps showing roads, or GPS coordinates, the real empty void of what is over the next hill or across the next border, was a serious undertaking, requiring commitment and attitude.

Tires—we know that the tire technology at the time was very poor. They did not have what was needed if a tire tube was ripped. They likely sewed it up. They did have patches. There was a way of laminating them where they actually lit them up after putting them on, then the glue over it, lighting the glue and the patch melted itself to the tire. It was actually a very efficient way of patching a hole.

I can identify with the tire problems Clancy must have faced, having had 26 flat tires on my journey around the world. It was something that happened probably to this guy at least weekly, having a flat tire and to patch it up. And of course he didn't have electric compressors or anything like that; he likely had a hand pump and had to get the tire blown up by pumping air by hand. It would likely almost become part of a daily routine. He would have had a lot of patches, possibly a lot of extra rubber that he could use to make his own patches, and also a sewing kit for the actual tires themselves, to stitch up rips or tears.

Gasoline—I would imagine it would have been a bigger logistical problem than the tires. He likely had tires sent out ahead of him, to stopping points. As for gasoline, we have to remember everywhere he went, and especially colonial areas at the time, the infrastructure of the roads would have been pretty fair. For instance, like in Africa, because of the camel trains or the trade route right across there had been established for centuries, so I don't see that finding gasoline was a great problem, because in every settlement somebody would have had a generator or something with a gasoline-driven engine that he could have gotten some fuel with. And I'll bet as well that, with that Henderson engine, he could have cut a lot of that gasoline with kerosene as well, and it probably would have run all right.

Transport across water—that would have probably been the easiest part of the trip. Shipping was a coming form of travel at the time. He would have gone down to the docks to say that he wanted to ship something and sometimes he could probably work his way across the water on the same ship. It was often that travelers would work as a cook, or down in the engineering spaces. He could add that in exchange for his work he would like them to strap his motorcycle on the fantail and he would sleep on the deck. If bad weather were to hit he could stay in the kitchen or engineering spaces. That was quite a common way for guys to get around on those old tramp steamers.

Health and medical—obviously if he broke himself out in the desert somewhere or in any of these countries, he would have had a serious problem. First of all, the medical system of any country at the time, even America, was very basic then compared to what is around now. When a person got hurt, he or she got hurt. If they had a serious wound, they had a serious problem, a much bigger problem than we would likely have today. But the people at the time would live with that. They didn't think and look at life quite the way we do. They didn't carry a bag of medicine everywhere they went. They just went and managed life along their route as best they could, far different from today when we have medical evacuation and travel health insurance to cover us.

Sleeping—Clancy would have slept outside when he couldn't find indoor sleeping. This is something that I can really relate to, being like a wandering vagrant, just like I am when I travel. I don't know about him, but I don't like being around people at night. I find isolated areas. He would have had to be prepared to tough it out under a tarp or on a bench when he could not sleep in a hotel, it was just a part to travel at the time, especially the way he went, by motorcycle.

That brings to question the matter of security. At this time travelers could carry firearms, anywhere in the world. And I would have bet this guy had at least a revolver with him that he could have protected himself with. I've read tales of other travelers that carried rifles and revolvers and it was never an issue when they crossed borders. A man made his own security.

Food—I also don't think eating would have been a big issue for him. Hard-stick salami has been around forever, as well as egg noodles and pasta, they don't go rotten, it doesn't matter if it's 110 degrees or if it's below zero. If he had those two things with a bit of water he was going to eat. He could have bought his food at public markets, just like the locals did.

Money—gold and US dollars is likely what he carried. Gold was gold, wherever he would have gone, so I can see him having some with him. Banks were around and he could exchange gold or US dollars, or even bank drafts. I can see money as being more of a non-problem than we look at it today, where we are caught up in electronic dependency, things like ATM's and credit cards.

Camera equipment—I suspect he would have had to set it up, possibly by winding it up, and then it went zzzztttt. To send the pictures home he would have had to find someplace in a city to have the film developed before sending the pictures to the publisher in New York. I suspect it was a time-consuming process, not only taking the pictures, but getting them developed and sent by mail.

Grit and determination—these two men, before they started out and during the first part of their trip, had a sense of adventure. From what I've read I don't think his friend, Storey, was fully prepared how great the adventure was. Obviously Storey wasn't a motorcyclist to start with and it seems he just didn't have the bottle for it, I mean, the falling off and having Clancy come back and ride the motorcycle, it just didn't sound like Storey was a man with a lot of pride and determination. I can only guess though. Then when he left Clancy, who knows, maybe he wrote a letter home to have a "Come home" letter catch up with them saying, "Hey, call me home," and he then had a way to weasel out of the rest of the journey. But if he really wanted to make the adventure and stay with his friend he would have. He didn't. What I do see as being devastating was when Clancy got used to traveling with Storey, you know for better or worse, he would have been used to him, and it's like the devil you know. When Storey left, there's a part of Clancy that was gone, and he was truly on his own. We have all traveled with people we got along well with and we've

4

been through some hard stuff—the weather, the road, living conditions, border crossings, a lot of uncertainty, and we come to learn how much we can depend on the other person, how much of the load they can carry. Then one day you say goodbye, and you never see each other again. A part of you goes with them, and then you're traveling differently. We have to learn to handle that emptiness well because that is who we are, but it still would have been tough for Clancy to soldier on alone once Storey left. But at the same time, we have had it happen to us a number of times and we just carry on alone, no problem, whereas he didn't start out to be a lone traveler. He had to make an incredible adjustment. We have also seen from what the man did afterwards that he was not the type of guy to quit under any circumstances, unless he was killed. This guy Clancy would have done the ride around the globe no matter what, because when he put his mind to something, if he felt it was worthwhile, he was in, boots and all. You can see from his record afterwards Clancy was an achiever. And when he put his mind to something he did it.

If I met Clancy today I would be proud if he shook my hand. I can only wish I'd had that opportunity. He was a real motorcycle adventurer, the likes of such we'll likely never see again. Times are different, roads and politics vastly changed, and the challenges he faced cannot be found today. He had one great ride around the world and I'm glad to have had a part in bringing it to print and the rest of the world by being part of this publication, an adventure in itself. I am glad Greg saw to it that Clancy did finally get the book in print, a major accomplishment on the part of Greg to get it done, and of course for Clancy having made the ride and given us his words. I say "Good job!" to both of them.

www.davebarr.com

PROLOGUE
Will Girdle the Globe on Motorcycles

(Published in the Fall of 1912 in
The Bicycling World and Motorcycle Review)

"Around the world on a motorcycle?" "Impossible," says one. "Insane idea," says another. "You'll have to wait till the Atlantic freezes over," exclaims a third—but my partner and I, well, we hold different views. It all depends upon your point of view. Old Mother Earth has been circled by almost everything at one time or another. Sailing craft, steamships, railway trains, bicycles, pedestrians and motorcars have all had their turn. Nothing remains but the airship, the submarine and the motorcycle—and now we are going to give the motorcycle a chance.

On the American Line steamer "Merion," sailing from Philadelphia, October 5, is Walter Storey, of the People's Institute, and myself, an advertising man, both enthusiastic motorcyclists, with Dublin as our destination, to start upon the longest, most difficult, and most perilous motorcycle journey ever attempted.

We are not undertaking this extensive trip for pleasure or adventure merely, our aim is to chart and map the first complete Motor Route Around the World for both motorcycles and automobiles—this route to include not simply the best roads between principal cities, but running directions for visiting the out-of-the-way point of historical and political interest in each country as well.

WALTER STOREY, MOVING PICTURE EXPERT.

Our route as laid out now covers fourteen European, one African and four Asiatic countries, besides including the Philippines, Hawaii and a new transcontinental route back from the Pacific. Our mileage in Europe will be about 5,500, in Africa 400, in Asia 5,000, in the United States and dependencies 3,500—a total of 14,000 miles on land besides 15,000 on water—all to be covered in one year.

CARL S. CLANCEY, ADVERTISING WRITER.

As few of our friends and business acquaintances can understand why we should desire to carry out this record-breaking journey, I believe that a few words explaining the cause of our ambition will be valued by our skeptical brothers in the motorcycle fraternity.

The facts are these: We are ordinary business men who are supersaturated with work and who have decided to invest a year's time in something else than the everlasting chase for the almighty dollar. Still as the year must pay its own expenses, our problem of how to use it to best advantage—of how to make the year the most effective and productive—was finally solved only by the plan to make the first motorcycle tour of the world and to chart the first complete motor route around the earth. This plan alone solved our requirements of outdoor life, originality and educational value.

As we must pay part of our expenses by writing articles for American and foreign magazines and newspapers enroute, and by publishing a complete book upon our return, we plan to lend a novel interest to the tour by taking along a complete camp equipment and by camping out whenever possible instead of following the example of everyone else and visiting hotels. To gain official recognition and co-operation for our efforts, besides also increasing our income, we have identified ourselves actively and permanently with the world wide good roads movement and the promotion of both international and interstate touring by charting the pioneer motor highway around the globe. We will encourage long distance touring at every opportunity.

In order to make the trip of the greatest value to American motorcyclists, the Bicycling World and Motorcycle Review has appointed me their special foreign correspondent, and will publish illustrated articles each month, outlining our adventures and discoveries enroute from the practical standpoint.

That is, we will prepare intimate record of each detail of our expenses during the entire year, lodging, food, gasoline, tires, repairs, etc. Ascertain and report on road conditions, licensed motor laws, speed limitations, customs regulations, hotel, garage and supply facilities and treatment, attitude toward motorcyclists, road guide systems, distances, character of gasoline and oil, tire supply, photographic supply, and every scrap of information of value to motorists who follow our track in the future. These facts will all be included with the illustrated account of our experiences.

The equipment that we have chosen for the trip—which by the way will cost us at least $4,000—is merely illustrative of the care we have taken to insure the success of our strenuous journey. First of all, we are to use two four-cylinder Henderson motorcycles, equipped with 29 x 2¾-inch Goodyear non-skid tires, Persons saddles, Veeder cyclometers, special luggage carriers, full assortment of extra parts, and a complete set of the tools necessary to overhaul the machines enroute. Two suits of Nathan's "Koveralls" are depended upon to protect us from rain and cold. A folding typewriter will help out in preparing our manuscripts, and large fountain pens will be used to take our notes. In addition to the foregoing a fine camera with an anastigmat lens has been added to the equipment, and a medicine kit practically completes the necessities.

Pains have been taken to insure an adequate supply of tires, gasoline and lubricating oil throughout the entire journey. As Europe is well dotted with supply stations, Egypt, India, Burmah, China and Japan were our only concern. To make sure of our tire supply we have arranged with the Goodyear Tire and Rubber Company to ship to us at various points, but the gasoline and oil problem necessitated letters to U. S. Consuls in the principal Asiatic and oriental centers in addition to lengthy consultations with the Standard and Vacium oil companies before adequate arrangements were made.

Mr. Storey also interviewed the Chinese consul in New York, with the view of ascertaining conditions to be met with in China. With characteristic oriental skill the wily son of Confucius did most of the interviewing, and if he knew anything of the land of the Golden Dragon he was not willing to disclose it, so we had to obtain our principal Chinese information from an American merchant who was visiting in New York after a 14-year sojourn in the Celestial Republic—we almost said Empire, from long custom.

Books covering India and Japan have led us to believe that the only obstacles to be conquered in these countries will be poor roads, so we are now trusting in the transportation of five gallon cans of gasoline on our luggage carrier to extend our present gas capacity of 150 miles to the length dictated by necessity. However, we may have to have gasoline shipped by rail or boat to a few isolated points.

Two months of steady work have been required to prepare for this tour and twelve will be needed to complete it. Here's hoping none will be required to recover from it!

CHAPTER I
Globe Girdlers A-Tour in Ireland

With Dublin as a Starting Point Donegal on the Northwest Coast is the Magnet That Allures—The Country's Peculiar Charm

So little is known by motoring America about the attractions of the land of many of its forefathers—Old Erin—that we decided to place it first upon our list of globe-girdling explorations. Finding that nothing heavier than a trunk can be landed at Queenstown, we had our two Hendersons shipped direct from the factory in Detroit to Dublin, via Liverpool, under the direction of Oelrichs & Co., New York forwarding agents. The machines were carefully boxed separately and the transportation cost was $20 delivered in Dublin ($10 express Detroit to New York, $5.50 ocean freight, $4.50 storage, carting, insurance, and forwarding charges).

Valuing comfort more than speed, we sailed on the one-class American liner "Merion" from Philadelphia October 5 and landed at Liverpool the morning of October 17, after a remarkably calm and warm voyage.

Both of us proved to be good sailors and did justice to our six English meals—six course breakfast at 8:00 AM, bouillon and crackers served on deck at 11:00, seven course luncheon at 1:00, afternoon tea at 4:00, eight course dinner at 6:30, and a supper of coffee, crackers and cheese at 9:00. It is small wonder that each of us gained over five pounds and began to crack such jokes as these: Noticing a bell-buoy in the Irish Channel, I said to Storey: "How do these bell-buoys make a living? I don't see any hotels around here." "Why, don't you see?" was his prompt reply. "They get 'tipped' by the waves!"

On the Voyage to Liverpool and Dublin Bay.

Finding the boat a delightfully unconventional place, we soon made friends with two charming Irish girls, who later adopted us as brothers, mended our clothes, and embroidered two fine flags bearing the legend "Around the World" for us to fly on our machines. The captain also proved to be a very jolly old tar, who showed us how to calculate altitudes with the barometer we brought along to forecast the weather, and conducted a miniature grand ball on deck one evening, with a Victrola for music, at our request. Our passage (run of the whole ship) and four-berth room totalled only $50, and $2.50 for tips.

As there is little of historic interest in Liverpool, we spent the day waiting for the night boat to Dublin in the neighboring old Roman town of Chester—the finest historical gem in all England, which we will describe more fully later—and purchased berths and passage to Dublin for $3.25 each.

We woke up along the quays of Dublin next morning to find our machines—sent by a fast White Star liner a week earlier—had not arrived on account of the habitual congestion of the far-famed and busy Liverpool docks.

We spent the day profitably, however, exploring the commanding public buildings of Dublin, where we found nearly everything at least 50 years behind the times; visiting the old Irish Houses of Parliament, now used as the Bank of Ireland; feasting our eyes upon the famous illuminated "Book of Kells" in the library of Trinity College, the leading Protestant university of Ireland, and purchasing an outfit of woollen underclothes and waterproof shoes and gloves—all of which proved no cheaper and less satisfactory than New York goods. We also registered our machines at the Dublin City hall and secured licenses for all Great Britain for a total of ten shillings ($2.40) each for the part of 1912 still remaining, $4.80 being the charge for a full year.

IN THE TOWN OF BALLYSHANNON WITH
DONEGAL BAY IN THE DISTANCE.

The editor of the "Irish Cyclist" supplied us with McCreedy's road maps and laid out our route to the West Coast for us the next morning, after which we spent the day uncrating and assembling our machines, which had finally arrived.

Petrol, as gasoline is known here, to fill our tanks cost 1 shilling and 7 pence (38 cents) per gallon, and this proved to the universal price throughout Ireland, Scotland and England. Vacuum lubricating oil is sold everywhere for 4s. 6d. (1.08) per gallon, 2s. 6d. per half gallon and 1s. 6d. per quart, in individual tins.

Some Experiences in Ireland's Historic Capital.

As Mr. Storey had never ridden a motorcycle (and as some people thought it queer that he should start around the world upon one without some little experience), I spent the next afternoon teaching him "how" in the famous Phoenix Park, near Dublin. By dark he had mastered his steed completely, but we were compelled to leave our machines in a nearby house till morning, having no carbide in our lamps, and learning that the Dublin "bobbies" are very strict in enforcing the lighting law, and even bicycles must all carry lights at night.

As we were starting off the next day a beautiful specimen of a gigantic, almost wax "Bobbie" held us up because we had no number plates on our front mudguard, and would have arrested us had we not been planning to leave town immediately. It took the rest of the day to have these plates fitted and painted with our numbers, "R. I. 2016—7," but after being photographed by an enterprising newspaper man (with a typical Irish breath) the following morning, started gaily off for Donegal.

Dublin had not finished with us, however, for before we had gone a block one of those two-story, bob-tail tram-cars which are universal in Great Britain, coming from behind another, ran smash into Mr. Storey, demolished his rear wheel, threw him to the pavement, ripped off the starting-crank casting, bent the handlebars and front fork badly—but allowed Storey to escape with a sorely bruised thigh.

An eager crowd of loafers carried the wrecked machine (making its mud-stained "Around the World" pennant appear sadly ironical) to a nearby shop, and refused to disperse until paid doubly for their efforts. Here we found the machine could be repaired, to our great relief, without cabling the factory for new parts.

OUR ROUTE THROUGH THE EMERALD ISLE.

Nothing daunted, I took Mr. Storey on in front on my machine, and, with 75 pounds of baggage on my carrier, made a third and triumphal start the following noon. In spite of the numerous herds of cattle and flocks of sheep which continually blocked the road, we covered 88 miles before dark, at 5:30.

Just outside of Dublin we saw our first thatched roof, whitewashed stone cottage, and after that met few shingled or tiled roofs until we reached Belfast. Newton-Butler, the quaint town whose Temperance Inn or "Cyclists' Rest" sheltered us and our machine the first night and fed us twice for a total of 6s. 6d. ($1.56), used thatch even on its two-story town hall.

ON THE PROW OF THE GOOD SHIP "MERION"

Finding our gasoline nearly gone the next morning, I spent an hour trying to buy some in the town, but found no "patrol," as the natives called it, that kerosene had never been heard of, and that no alcohol outside of whiskey could be bought. I finally purchased a pint of "paraffine oil"—which is used wherever house lamps can be afforded, instead of the universal tallow candle—mixed this with the cupful of gas I had and safely reached Lisnaskal, a more favored town, four miles away. Here our steed drank its fill of the precious liquid called Pratt's Motor Spirit, which is a refined product of the Standard Oil Co., of a much higher grade than its American variety, and is sold in two-gallon tins at 38 cents a gallon by small shops and hotels in every other town we have visited in Great Britain.

On Our Way to the Rocky Donegal Coast.

The kindly officers of the Royal Irish Constabulary, who have barracks in every Irish town, were all good sports, never questioning our speed, and often took great pains to direct us accurately. Not so one shy road-worker, however (one of those ancient men who spend their time keeping their allotment of highway in order), who, when we were approaching a forked road, called out "straight ahead" in answer to our inquiry for the best road to take. We found all the roads good in Ireland, however, many being "steam rolled," especially in the northern part, even to the tiniest road through enormous peat or "turf" bogs. But the Irish roads are not well drained, and as it rains very often their surface, no matter how hard underneath, frequently is very soft and decorated with slippery pools of water.

ALL READY FOR THE START FROM DUBLIN.

There are no hills in central Ireland, and nothing to lower our average of 20 miles per hour, except the numbers of cattle or sheep traveling to market, which we met everywhere; the tiny donkeys, with their two-wheeled toy carts, which seemed to much prefer the wrong side of the road, and the hens, ducks and turkeys which invariably did their utmost to commit suicide under our wheels in their insane desire to beat us home. Every farm house kept its hens in the road, and the miracle that we haven't killed a single hen (only one dog—in Scotland) is due to the fact that we found the best procedure was to rush through them and get past before they had time to get homesick.

The second day we had two bad falls in slippery ditches, when dodging some deaf man's cart—and deafness seems very prevalent in Ireland—but were able to go on each time. We were delighted to find that the railway gates are locked across the railroad tracks instead of the road, forcing the trains to wait for traffic instead of vice versa, as in the United States.

Hearing that civil war was imminent between north and south Ireland, and after backing out of several violent Home Rule discussions, we decided to be prepared for the worst; so, before entering Ulster, we got out our Savage automatics and, to practice, banged away at a tree on the lonely roadside, beside the beautiful Lough Erne. This precaution proved unnecessary, although it is certain that an outbreak will occur in Ulster in case the Home Rule bill passes. In Dublin we were told, on the other hand, that there would be fighting if it didn't pass, so we await developments.

Ancient Donegal, the mountainous northwest county of Old Erin, the most Irish part of all Ireland, by far the most wildly beautiful part—and the main thing we came to Ireland to see—entranced us during our third day's travel. Here, far from the tourist's contamination, amid bold, treeless hills of terrific height, the older people speak Gaelic (the children both Gaelic and English), live in tiny stone huts perched in the barren, heather-covered, wind-swept valleys, and represent the extreme in poverty. Here a donkey is an unheard-of luxury, and even hens are very scarce. Every family raises one pig a year, which is sold to pay the rent—never eaten. On the day we entered the far west district we passed about 40 enormous, pink, tired pigs on their way to the annual fair or market day for that section.

NATIVE DWELLING PLACE IN COUNTY DONEGAL

CHAPTER II
Globe Girdlers A-Tour in Ireland

***

Splendid Coast Scenery of Donegal is Awe-Inspiring—Wonderful Cliffs and the Giants' Causeway

But the awe-inspiring bleakness of Donegal's mountains and the blending richness of the indescribable coloring of its whole countryside, is the secret of Donegal's charm. Leaving our machines in the walled-in yard of a tiny, one-roomed hut, the home of a fisherman, his wife and five children—devoid of furniture except a plate rack and one bed, we started up the mountain to view the famous cliffs of Sliene League, with the eldest boy for our guide. Finding him a very intelligent chap, although clothed in rags, we questioned him, and discovered that, although he had never been to the next town, ten miles from home, he was well up in Irish history, and could tell us the height of Niagara Falls!

After climbing over numberless "turf" holes, which these peasants rent from the landlord (who owns not only the whole town but the whole country) along with their hut and plot of ground, past lonely huts in narrow valleys, with their rounding, thatched roofs laced down to strong pegs in the walls by a network of twisted straw or plaited pine ropes to hold them and their straw chimneys from flying off in the wind, we finally reached the top of the 1,000-foot cliffs of Bungles, from which we looked across a tiny bay upon the stupendous 2,000-foot face of the famous Sliene League mountain—a bald, sheer precipice upon whose crest clouds rested lightly, upon whose base the full, unbroken swell of the broad Atlantic broke with the roar of despair.

Speechless we stood for several minutes. Nothing but the echoing roar of the surf broke the deathly silence of ages and ages. We fancied ourselves on the moon—not a tree, not a bird, not a living thing broke upon the awful solitude and vastness of the place. Surely here was the place to get in tune with the Infinite—to come to die! We threw a stone over the face of our cliff; it took seven seconds to reach the foaming water far a way at our feet. We raised our eyes and there, for 40 miles, both north and south, stretched a broken series of tremendous headlands and precipices. Upon Carrigan Head, to our left, nearby, an old square signal tower, built by the English in Napoleon's time, jutted against the sky, while far to the north we could just discern another—lone, desolate, forgotten—a monument to fears that were happily never realized. To the west the Atlantic stretched unruffled to the setting sun. The grandeur, the absolute sublimity of the place was indescribable.

Reluctantly, silently, painfully, we drove ourselves back to the valley where we left our machine—almost profanely, for upon this day, the most perfect day of our entire stay in Ireland, the day when we wanted it most of all, we had left our camera behind at the hotel!

The brilliant moon enticed us on that night, and before we were halted in the queer little town of Ballybofe at nine o'clock by a very heavy mist, we had put 55 Irish miles (which are one-quarter longer than English miles) between us and the ancient Donegal coast.

We passed through Londonderry the next noon to cash one of our Thos. Cook & Son drafts, and by four o'clock reached the Giants' Causeway. Leaving our machines at a hotel (for, unlike Donegal, the Causeway is sadly commercialized), we descended a winding path along the face of the magnificent cliffs over a mile, when we were shocked to find ourselves confronted with an iron fence and charged sixpence admission to this remarkable freak of nature.

Our only consolation was the fact that, like Donegal and all Ireland, we had the vast cliffs all to ourselves and explored the inspiring heights and fantastic rock formations which form a fitting eastern wall for this romantic land, second only in grandeur to its western counterpart, Donegal.

GIANT'S CAUSEWAY (NORTHERNMOST IRELAND) AT FOUR O'CLOCK ON A RAINY OCTOBER AFTERNOON.

Returning to the Causeway proper (which is not nearly so wonderful as its neighboring cliffs and promontories) about 4:30, although it was raining, blowing in squally gusts, and very dark, we decided to attempt to get a picture. I climbed out onto the Causeway itself, while Storey tried a minute's exposure, with the great success you can see in the reproduction here.

At five o'clock it was practically dark, but we headed our machine south for some 40 miles down the coast. We had covered only 15 miles, however, before a terrific storm broke upon us in a mountain pass, soaking us to the skin, nearly blowing us over several times, and compelling us to return to the last town we had passed, Bally Castle in County Antrim, 3½ miles back. Here we were very glad to take shelter in the "Antrim Arms," and to give our machine credit for not misfiring once, in spite of the water, which gave me many most annoying electric shocks through my soaked leather gloves.

FARMLANDS ON THE EMERALD ISLE'S WEST COAST.

The fury of the storm spent itself in the night, but it continued to blow and rain all the next day, during which we followed the famous Antrim coast road 65 miles to Belfast, along the face of forbidding cliffs, through two short tunnels, and past several ancient castles, continually leaning against the gusty wind which drenched us with spray from the sea and always buffeting the sharp, stinging rain in our face. Although we reached Belfast by one o'clock, in time to catch a train, which we afterwards learned did not leave until 3:20, I found I had frozen both my ears, which have since scabbed out and given me the greatest annoyance.

Leaving Storey to rest up in Belfast, I continued to Dublin that evening on the queer English train and rode his repaired machine (which cost only £3 to make as good as new) back to Belfast, 100 miles, the next afternoon in 5½ hours—in time for us both to catch the night boat to Glasgow.

Altogether we covered 500 miles in Ireland in six days—400 miles on one machine. We had no engine or tire trouble of any kind and could not imagine a more enjoyable way to travel, especially as they say "the Irish trains, like cows' tails, are always behind." The roads were all hard and good, except in western Donegal, where they were often full of stones and sharp, steep curves. We met no hills, however, that one could not easily negotiate—in extreme cases slipping the clutch a little to relieve our motor of its double burden. We met several Gaelic sign posts in the north, but always found English posts on important turns.

Ireland is so quaint, so different from Scotland, England and America, so blessed with charming, picturesque hillsides of the most entrancing colors, and inhabited by the most fascinating people, that we urge every motorist to visit it—and especially Donegal—at his earliest opportunity. Next time we will spend two months instead of two weeks there.

CHAPTER III
From Glasgow to London and Rotterdam
Around the World on a Motorcycle

"Europe has been done to death—slide over it." As these were the encouraging words with which the editor-in-chief counselled my report on the first stages of our journey "tout le monde," as the French call it, it is with great humbleness that I select for these pages only the most interesting details of our trip through Scotland, England, Holland, Belgium, and Northern France.

Looking away back to Ireland over just one thousand miles of thrilling adventure, it seems impossible that only a month has passed since we drained our petrol tanks on the Belfast dock and shipped our machines at the last moment as excess baggage on the night boat for Glasgow.

As we slipped down the harbor past the great "Olympic," newly docked for the winter's repairs, our hearts were indeed heavy to leave human Old Erin, whose mists, a little more heavy than usual, seemed also to be weeping at our departure. The choppy sea in the Channel, however, soon turned our attention to a lower organ and forced a quick search for our berths.

After breakfasting on board the next morning for two shillings each, and paying $4.66 apiece for our own and our steeds' transportation, we spent the two hours waiting for the tide to rise in the Clyde sufficiently to enable the machines to be carried up the narrow gangplank, in ferreting out Thos. Cook & Sons' Glasgow office, reading our first mail from home and welcoming a fine Bartholomew's road map of Great Britain, which the Auto-Cycle Union sent us from London for $1.25.

Glasgow, even more than Belfast, reminded us of a hustling American city—but the people were—oh! so Scotchy! Unlike Dublin, where we met every type imaginable except typically Irish characters (concluding they had all gone to America), the Scotch race impressed us as being very individual, and supported our belief that it is the people, not the buildings, that make a city.

Especially distinctive is the Scotch accent, being almost unintelligible to us at times; while the little red-nosed, bare-kneed ladies who gathered about us whenever we stopped always rolled their "r's" and reproduced Harry Lauder's squeak to a T.

As we had brought our petrol along on the boat with us in a can (this being officially permissible), we were able to proceed to a paint-store, where we purchased a "fill" for the universal price of 1s. 7d., or 38 cents a gallon.

Storey, not having ridden since his Dublin accident, was my passenger through the heavy traffic to the city limits, while I returned for his machine, riding in on the narrow-gauged, double-decked trolley for only one cent—a new experience for me in street railway transportation rates.

FAMOUS "MARRIAGE CHURCH" AT GRETNA GREEN.

This delayed our departure for the south until almost dark, and in spite of the detailed directions from a well-meaning "bobby" with a typically Scotch breath, we soon lost our way in the gathering gloom, made almost infernal by the lurid glares of numerous near-buy iron foundries.

Finally we were forced to put up for the night at an unprepossessing inn called "The Black Bull," in the dreary town of Stonehouse. Inside, however, everything was bright and cheery and typically Scotch, as we learned later, in its spic and span-ness.

Instead of the peat, universal in Ireland, the glowing hearth of huge chunks of soft coal, mined nearby, was reflected by the shining pots and pans which decorated the walls of the reception-hall-kitchen, and lighted up the polished flagstone floor, bordered with fancy chalk designs to betray any dirt that might search for rest in its corners.

Tea, with meat, breakfast, and a big feather bed, cost us here $1.15 each. We were not charged for our machines, which were quartered in a stable, nor were we charged storage for them elsewhere, except in large cities.

Rising before daylight the next morning, we breakfasted with an Edinburgh clergyman, who told us that although he had been a weekly visitor at "The Black Bull" for several years, we were the first guests he had met; the bar being the inn's principal mainstay and pure whiskey its principal staple.

We had originally planned to go north from Glasgow through the Trossachs to Edinburgh, but delays in Ireland caused us to choose a more direct route to London, including the English Lake District, which we passed through that afternoon, during the latter part of our record day's run of 133 miles.

Through the Highlands and Over the English Border.

Splendid roads, often with stretches of asphalt, led us on, winding over heather covered moors and braes into the bold, bleak, southern "Hielands," dotted here and there with enormous flocks of woolly sheep, accompanied always by a lone, picturesque herdsman with a story-book "crook"; and whose bare, steep sides were continually broken by tiny waterfalls and deep ravines.

Leaving "Caledonia, stern and wild," we passed through many severe little villages to the border town of Gretna Green. Here we "snapped" the ugly wayside chapel, famous for its many memories of elopements and the exciting chases of ardent lovers by heartless English parents and guardians, during the years 1750 to 1800, when it was legal in Scotland for anyone to perform the marriage ceremony.

We passed through Carlisle, in England, a few miles further on, then turned southwest into the entrancingly beautiful English Lake District at Keswick.

OUR ROUTE FROM GLASGOW TO LONDON.

Coming suddenly over the brow of a well-graded hill, the full glory of a mad jumble of the towering Cumbrian mountains, bald of all trees except those protected in deep crevices, but rich with deep brown and purple heather burst upon our sight. Wild skylines of fantastically jagged summits faded mysteriously into the distance, partially hidden by a golden haze which rested on the air and transformed the whole district into fairyland.

Throwing out our clutches we glided silently down the winding road, presenting a new vista at every turn, and then continued slowly on past numberless silvery cascades racing down seemingly from the very cloud-tipped summits of the precipitous peaks, to the lovely lakes of Ullswater, Derwentwater, and Grassmere nestling below.

Although evidently a great tourist resort, we had the perfect roads and, in fact, practically the whole of romantic Westmoreland, all to ourselves; congratulating each other upon having come in the "off season," so that our dreams were not shattered by the foolish cries of summer tourists.

We spent that night at Windermere the southern railroad entrance to this charming land, and could then readily understand why Wordsworth, Coleridge, Southey and De Quincey, whose homes we passed that day, had found their life and inspiration here. Next to ancient Donegal, which we discovered in Ireland, the Cumbrian mountains form the garden spot of our travels.

"The Crown and Anchor," in Northwich, Cheshire, was our stopping place the following day, reached through the great steel and manufacturing cities of Lancaster, Preston, Wigan and Warrington, for the purpose of visiting the famous salt mine, which has undermined the whole town and causes frequent "depressions" of its buildings. Here large lakes have been known to disappear in one night, and many a burgher has awoke in the morning to find his second story bedroom window level with the street.

KESWICK, CAMBRIAN MOUNTAINS AND DERWENT WATER.

After securing official permission to inspect the mine, we were lowered in a cylindrical iron bucket, with our guide clinging to the chain above, 250 feet down a black shaft until a mammoth cave received us into a miniature nether world. All was blackness except where a flickering miner's taper lit up the side of one of the huge pillars left to support the vaulted ceiling some twenty-five feet above. Soon we were led up the terraced rock to one side, while a terrific blast not fifty feet away tore loose a carload of the dirty salt crystals from the opposite wall and left us gasping for breath, while the reverberating echoes died away in the caverns beyond. We were glad indeed to be hauled up again into sunshine and God's free air.

Picturesque Chester is in Class by Itself.

Seventeen miles west we came upon the old Roman walled town of Chester, crammed so full of quaint picturesqueness that we were surprised not to be charged admission. Indeed, ancient Chester and all its surroundings seemed to be picture-book land. Everywhere we looked was worth a photograph. The overgrown Christmas tree trains of cars, a number of toy lakes and candy-like horses in the trim patchwork fields we spied on our way, all harmonized to make us feel we had discovered Mother Goose land at last.

But aside from the high-gabled, half-timbered, picturesque buildings, emblazoned with gaudy coats of arms and honeycombed with endless second story arcades of tiny shops, the biggest attraction of Chester is its historic interest.

KING CHARLES' TOWER, CHESTER WALL.

Walking around the top of the walls which still encircle the city proper, we saw the heavy rings to which the old Roman and

Venetian ships were moored; sat at the same window where King Charles witnessed Cromwell's defeat of his army in the fields below, and stood solemnly in the crypt or "vaulted chamber" where De Quincey wrote his "Opium Eater."

MOUNTAINS AND ROAD IN ENGLISH LAKE DISTRICT.

Nowadays Chester is a residential suburb of Liverpool, living mainly in its glorious past and carefully perpetuating in its new buildings the unique style of its architecture, which we found, to our sorrow, nowhere else in England. For us Chester was the most interesting of all British towns—much more worth while for the American even than London.

Returning to Northwich for the night, we covered the seventeen miles in thirty minutes (for we found no speed traps in Great Britain), and continued the next day to Birmingham through the "Black Country" or coal mining district of England, uninteresting except for the queer names of hotels and public houses we passed. The ones we noted down include "The Hen and

Chicken," "The Lad in the Lane or the Green Man," "The Ring o' the Bells," "The Bee-Hive," "The Blue Boar," "The Swan with Two Necks," "The Malt Shovel," "The Dog and Duck," "The Six Ashes," and "The Brick Layer's Arms."

Visiting artist friends we met on the boat, we celebrated Election Day in "the States" and "Guy Fawkes's Day here by cleaning up and adjusting our machines and in draining some poor oil from the crankcases which we had once been forced to buy in place of Vacuum oil, which is sold in practically every bicycle shop and garage throughout Great Britain, in sealed quart, two-quart and gallon cans for 36 cents a quart and $1.08 a gallon.

We had no trouble in securing the high grade "Shell" and "Pratt's Motor Spirit" anywhere, the hotels of even the smallest town keeping a small supply always on hand.

A Tribute to the English Road System.

The roads are excellent and well drained throughout England, an important fact for us, as we often rode for hours in the rain. Usually, however, we would soon ride through a rainstorm, and being well protected and toughened by the outdoor life, paid no attention to the weather, much to the disgust of our barometer, which had been consulted so often on shipboard.

With the help of our large map, the numerous finger posts and frequently the courteous "AA" and "RAC" road guides who patrol the roads on bicycles in resort sections and never asked if we were "Members," we had little trouble in finding our way, except in large cities, where we were always delayed and often lost to each other. In fact, it was the favourite stunt for one of us to wait for the other who had already gone on ahead. Our heavy baggage was a constant annoyance, persisting in jarring loose when we were short of time; while our lamps, never fit for motorcycle work, were most exasperating. We urge every motorcyclist who travels on short winter days, which ended our daylight at 4:30, to buy the largest and strongest lamps he can carry, regardless of cost.

ST. WERBURGH STREET, CHESTER, SHOWING CATHEDRAL.

Throughout England, and especially in Birmingham, where one of the new English makes is produced, along with practically every other metal article invented, we saw many short, noisy, belt-driven English machines, but rarely without a side car attached to it. Although most machines over here seem to have but one cylinder, they usually have two or three-speed gears and handle the exceedingly popular side car with apparent ease. We saw several "cycle cars" or tiny automobiles, seating two tandem fashion, and learned that they are assured a big future. We have met nothing outside of a full-grown touring car that we would exchange for our Hendersons, however, which have never failed to draw appreciative crowds wherever we stopped, our surprisingly fat Goodyear tires forming the side-show.

The only object of unusual interest in Birmingham, the magnificent Elizabethan manor house, "Aston Hall," built in 1541, well repaid our visit before continuing sixteen miles south to the romantic ruins of Kenilworth Castle. We wandered about this imposing mediæval pile of the Plantagenet era for an hour, realizing how helpless books and photographs really are to convey the actual atmosphere of a place.

Warwick Castle, which we saw from the outside four miles further on, is much the same kind of a fortress in a state of preservation that Kenilworth is in ruins. We had jokingly planned to call upon the mistress of this feudal stronghold, Lady Warwick, accepting an invitation which she gave to her entire audience during a lecture on "Suffrage" which we heard in Brooklyn last winter; but finding that her ladyship was out of town, we continued fourteen miles along the Avon to peek at Shakespeare's fenced in, commercialized old home.

After my being delayed by a bad fall, caused by dodging an automobile coming from behind a team on the wrong side of the road, we succeeded in reaching Oxford at 5:30, making our total 70 miles for the day.

Three shilling and sixpence each secured separate beds for us in the old commercial hotel "Roebuck," and four shillings provided us both with thick English chops for dinner. We usually ate a cake of milk chocolate for our noonday lunch on the road, and as the English have their dinner at noon, we always had to order special dishes—except in London—to get anything hot (besides the universal tea) at night.

38

A Glimpse at the Prince of Wales at Oxford.

After visiting the most noted of Oxford's twenty-one ancient colleges the next morning, reveling in their elaborate time-scarred architecture, beautiful chapels and quiet quadrangles, we were lucky enough to meet the Prince of Wales face to face! Although escorted by his tutor and guarded by a detective upon a bicycle, we had a good look at the future King of England—a rosy, undeveloped boy of eighteen, now a "Fresher" in Magdalen College, whom we should have passed unnoticed had it not been for the excited antics of our guide.

CLOISTERS AND TOWER, MAGDALEN COLLEGE, OXFORD.

As the colleges are scattered throughout the city, and although each one is equipped to bestow all the usual degrees, the students often attend several different colleges at a time, going about from lecture to lecture in abbreviated black capes, cut to devote their rank, on bicycles by the hundreds and motorcycles by the scores.

After having my front forks straightened, we succeeded in covering 54 miles, to London, by six o'clock, but had to omit Henley-on-Thames and Windsor Castle on the 57-mile route to do it.

MESSRS. CLANCY AND STOREY ARRIVE IN LONDON.

Leaving our machines at a garage in West Kensington, we rode in to the Strand on top of a motor 'bus, past Hyde Park, Oxford Circus, Pall Mall, Trafalgar Square, Piccadilly, and all those short-story names, to Surrey street, between the Strand and the Thames Embankment. Here a quiet commercial hotel sheltered us, instead of the much finer but no more expensive New Strand Palace Hotel, which the automobile show had filled to overflowing. The next morning we braved the dense traffic and brought our machines safely to the store of the Robertson Motor Co., the Henderson London agency, on Great Portland street, where they were put upon exhibition in the show window and saved us garage charges.

Having taken out membership in the Auto-Cycle Union of England before leaving New York, we sought out its headquarters at 89 Pall Mall, and were delighted to find it located in the magnificent building of the Royal Automobile Club.

Here we were welcomed cordially and given the privileges of associate membership in the "RAC," the use of a large library and writing room, and the services of the entire staff of the "RAC" route experts in providing us with maps, road information, and in laying out our route clear to China.

It took several days for these facts and our international passes to be prepared, after we had demonstrated our ability to ride before the "RAC" examiner, who also officially identified our machines; yet the cost was only $2.50 each for our passes, 30 cents each for our "G. B." number plates, and $1.25 apiece for our maps of England, Central Europe and Italy. The clubroom privileges were worth that alone.

While it is not necessary to join the Union for a tour of the British Isles, a good map being sufficient for directions, for Continental travel its help is practically invaluable; yet touring membership costs but five shillings.

Although we were not treated to a single "London fog" during our stay, a week was enough for us, for there is really little of great interest here. The automobile show at Olympia compared favourably with similar exhibitions in New York, Boston and Paris, however, and we were sorry not to be able to stay for the "Cycle Show," two weeks later.

We also took in the Houses of Parliament, where the Peers were having a grand rough house over the Home Rule bill; the amusing horse guards at Whitehall; the ugly Buckingham Palace, where the King keeps house, at the end of the Mall; the National Gallery, the Old curiosity Shop, London Tower, and were fortunate enough to connect with the annual Lord Mayor's Parade, which looked to us like a rich burlesque of the coronation.

But London did not appeal to us, not because of its grimy, old-fashionedness, but because of the cold-blooded life of the simple, self-contained English people; so different from the "push" of New York and the vigorous vivacity of the Parisian.

It was not easy to leave London, however, for although we started early Saturday morning to ride our machines to the Custom House to catch the Rotterdam boat at noon, the slimy asphalt caused repeated falls, one of which broke off my starting crank housing, and finally compelled us to have our machines carted to the Fenchurch Station, where we put them on the boat train for Tilbury, the passenger landing for the Batavier Line.

We eventually succeeded in getting them and ourselves aboard the night boat for Rotterdam, after first loading them on the tender which plies from the wharf to mid-channel.

To partially make up for this extra expense, which loading at the Custom House would have avoided, we bought second-class tickets and managed to be comfortable after eating a lukewarm meal which the steward found somewhere in the other end of the boat. Altogether, it cost us $9 to get ourselves and $6 to get our machines from London to Rotterdam. Next time we will cross from Harwich to The Hook.

CHAPTER IV
From Rotterdam to Paris

"**G**AI PAREE," Jan. 15.—Upon landing in Rotterdam, we had to wait two hours on the dock in the rain, amusing ourselves watching the quaint, long-bearded policemen (who must have found it difficult to take themselves seriously), while the customs officer was roused out of bed. We were further cheered by having to pay $1.08 for Sunday examination of our passes, which eliminated all customs deposits, however.

The queer Dutch money, for which we exchanged some good English gold in London, did not bother us long, for two American cents equal five Dutch in value, and forty cents one gulden. So a fill of "autolene" at one gulden per gallon started us north for Amsterdam at noon. Getting out of Rotterdam we lost each other, as usual, blaming it this time on the guttural Dutch accent; but finally met in Delft, the famous pottery center, half way to The Hague.

The bumpy, uneven brick roads were so bad we felt we deserved pay for using them; yet here we met our first (but only) tollgate, and it cost us each three cents to get by. Although the universal "ruwielpads" or cycle paths were always "ferboden" to "motorrutingen" such as ours, we slid into them at every opportunity, and thus were able to average a pretty good speed.

In spite of the fact that the Dutch roads are all sign-posted, we missed the main road outside of The Hague and took a dyke road following straight stretches of canals for miles at a time; past scores of huge, moss-covered windmills and spotless little hamlets squatting on the flat, green country stretching in monotonous sameness as far as we could see in every direction.

The land is often from six to ten feet below the water level of the canals, but the shell dyke road which is followed to Holfweigen, missing Haarlem altogether, was much more comfortable than the main roads of brick. From here an absolutely straight seven miles of brick road, bordered by a trolley line on each side, led us into Amsterdam by nightfall. Here a cordial young Dutchman, the Overland automobile agent for Holland, whom we had met on the Rotterdam boat, welcomed us at his garage and found us a comfortable room at the top of a flight of steep Dutch stairs in the Rembrant Hotel, for three shillings each, including breakfast.

Fifty-four miles of backbone churning had shaken our breakfast into a nutshell, and as we had not stopped for lunch we beat a hasty retreat to the Cosmopolitan restaurant "De Kroon," in Rembrantplein, "Telefoon, No. 2479." Here we enjoyed a tremendous table d'hote dinner for 1½ gulden, or 60 cents, ordering beer to avoid paying the extra charge of ten cents for our "cover" if we had not. Butter was also extra here, as we have found it to be everywhere on the Continent.

The main place of interest in Amsterdam, "The Venice of the North," is the Het Rijks Museum of Art, where, among an unrivalled collection of Flemish paintings, we gazed upon Rembrandt's famous "Night Watch," one of the finest works of the great master.

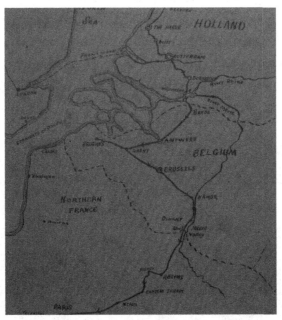

OUR ROUTE—HOLLAND, BELGIUM
AND NORTHERN FRANCE.

Returning to the garage, we found our machines all cleaned up, filled with gasoline and oil, and our tool bags supplied with "adapters" to enable us to fit metric thread spark plugs into our cylinders. For this service, the night's storage, and a detailed road map of the country to Antwerp, the generous Dutchman would accept no pay, except a short ride on my machine, which he greatly admired, and tips to his mechanics.

It was therefore with much regret that we bade him and fascinating Amsterdam adieu that afternoon, to follow the straight brick road through ancient Haarlem back to The Hague, the Dutch capital.

Here I was nabbed by a jolly "cop" because my lamp had gone out, but was allowed to proceed to the "American" Hotel, where, after lighting it again, he found I was a foreigner.

Having no convenient back yard, the lusty proprietor of this honored house sheltered our machines in his rather palatial front hall, no charge being made for this courtesy, in spite of the fact that they kept the sidewalk packed with a curious gathering through the evening.

SEVEN MILES STRAIGHT ROAD—HAARLEM TO AMSTERDAM.

Contrary to our plan, we were destined to spend two more nights in Queen Wilhelmina's "Netherland," for after passing through bustling Rotterdam the next noon, we struck our first pavie, which made life miserable until we left Brussels four days later.

HET RIJKS MUSEUM OF ART AT AMSTERDAM.

Covered with slimy mud tracked on by heavy two-wheeled carts from the field, the wretched pavement soon succeeded in throwing Storey into the ditch, when endeavouring to pass one of those numerous carts, whose drivers almost never condescended to hear our horns and rarely yielded an inch of the road when they did (not being "motor-educated," like the teamsters of France and England). The fall broke off his starting crank, several spokes in his rear wheel, and forced us to creep along until I ran out of gasoline, and had to return a mile to a bicycle shop, where the precious spirit was on sale.

Rain and darkness finally stalled us at Zwinjdrecht, where we found shelter at the "Het Witte Paard," a combination hotel, café and amusement hall.

New York Price for a Dutch Breakfast.

To avoid extra charges, we always made it a practice to secure detailed prices on both meals and bed, written down, before engaging accommodations. As we were usually mistaken for Englishmen, this plan worked very well. The garcon here, however, who had once been a steward on the Holland-American Line and could get away with a little English, recognized our American identity, after posting some of our letters home that evening. He must have owned stock in the establishment, for he laid low for us the next morning with a charge of 40 cents apiece for breakfast of bread and chocolate and 30 cents each for two small chops in addition.

Not being satisfied with the explanation that meat was always "extra," I demanded to see the proprietor, whom, I was informed, had made up the outrageous bill. This request being flatly refused on the grounds that his highness was still asleep, I calmly halved the breakfast item with my pen, laid down the exact change for the new total and started for the door—ignoring the volley of threats and protests meanwhile.

But not so fast! The furious waiter reached it before me, locked it fast and, for greater effect, pocketed the key. Being in no hurry, as the ferryboat needed to take us across the river had not put in an appearance, I quietly told the childish man that, while we would pay New York prices in New York, we would never put up with them in Holland, and started to hunt up the proprietor.

This was too much for the garcon's pride, but after relieving his mind of a few choice opinions of Americans in general, he swapped the key for his tip, and we marched out triumphant, just in time to catch the ferry for Dordrecht.

New spokes were made up for Storey here, but an hour and three-quarters' wait for the "hourly" ferry across the bay from Willemsdorp to Moerdyck, where the Rhine enters the North Sea, seven miles south from Dordrecht, and a long struggle with slimy pavie, landed us for the night at the queer little inn of Zundert—the southernmost town in Holland—with only 24 miles to our credit.

BELGIAN VENDOR, DOG CART, AND GENDARME.

In spite of its poor roads, we were sorry to leave Holland the next morning. It is so picturesque and free from artificiality! It is true that we were shocked by seeing the sedate small boys solemnly puffing on big cigars and man-size pipes, in spite of their tender years of eight or ten, and especially so to see a pretty girl escorted by her soldier lad stoop down in the middle of the road to tie up his shoelace! It made our hearts ache, also, to see the noble dogs, sometimes four abreast, strain in their harness in front of, but more often underneath, the heavy carts. They were always splendid pullers, but still dogs, however, for they seldom lost an opportunity to bark at us; and many are the old ladies we have had to dodge because of their inability to steer their canine tractors.

Holland Picturesque and Free from Artificiality.

We saw wooden shoes everywhere in Holland and often in Belgium, as they are much more serviceable than leather upon the moist ground. Although they are painted inside and out and whitewashed every morning, they are never worn inside the spotless houses. Dutch cleanliness is no fairy tale either, for we passed through our hamlet where the energetic housewives were actually scrubbing the cobblestone street with soap and water. We saw none of those "typically" wide Dutch trousers and only a few specimens of the women's "national" headdress, but understand that Thos. Cook & Son maintain a colony on the Isle of Marken in the Zuider Zee where these old-fashioned styles are still worn for the benefit of tourists.

FAMOUS BELFRY TOWER IN ANCIENT BRUGES.

Holland is really a German province in its character and customs, while Belgium, or "Belgique," is decidedly French. But, unlike the Dutch, Belgians have no national language and no distinct national coinage.

Not knowing that the word "douane" meant "customs," we almost got into trouble upon entering Belgium by riding gaily past the frontier station. A gendarme captured us and brought us back to the irate officer in charge, who gave us a good idea of the French power of expression before he had expended his fury into our smiling faces, and discovered that we had not understood a word of his masterly denunciation. Our placid ignorance finally disgusted him so that he stamped our passes and sent us on, merely grafting 40 cents apiece for a "police pass" that was never looked at.

From Breda, the first town of any size in north Belgium, two roads lead to Antwerp—the regular automobile route via Hoogstraeten, and an absolutely direct one five miles shorter. Hoping to save time, we chose the latter, being informed that a cycle path ran the whole 34 miles, and made splendid time until driven on to the impossible huge blocks of wretched pavie by a heartless gendarme.

The Omniprescent Gendarme of Belgium

Unlike Holland, where we saw none outside of cities, there are hundreds of military gendarmes in Belgium; so fear of delay from arrest kept us bumping along in agony, until we came upon a gang of road builders who had left a level trail clear to Antwerp. They were so welcome that we photographed them, but, like most of our cameratic attempts, the light was too poor for success.

We spent an hour in the mighty port of Antwerp hunting for a bridge over the "Lazy Scheldt" which our map indicated on the road to Ghent, and which everyone glibly directed us to. At last we discovered that no such bridge ever existed and took a ferryboat across. We reached Ghent (or "Gand") via St. Nicholas, as we usually did our daily stopping place, long after dark, but were very fortunate to find the well equipped shop of Joseph Houard & Fils, 11 Rue des Vanniers, where we left our machines, and continued by rail that evening to Brughes, deciding to "give in" to the pavie for one day at least.

"November 22nd, Red Letter Day" —as recorded in my diary—was spent visiting the treasures of historic Brughes (one of the greatest commercial centers of the Middle Ages), by many considered to be of deeper interest than those of Paris or London.

CUSTOMS OFFICIALS AT BELGIAN-FRENCH BOUNDARY.

Here we saw, in the Cathedral of St. Saueur, high mass being celebrated in exactly the same form and precisely the same place that it has been for nearly a thousand years past; priceless paintings of world-famous masters hanging in the original chapels for which they were designed; the carved figures decorating the entire front of the Hotel d'Ville, or town hall, built in 1376, which attracted us inside to glory in the inexpressible charm of the rich Gothic meeting hall—a dream in red and gold; the ancient Chapel of the Holy Blood; the remarkable carved wood chimney piece "du Franc" that ornaments the Palais de Justice; the huge church of Notre Dame, whose 350-foot spire has always been the first landmark seen by sailors from the Spanish Main; and the gigantic old belfry, the object of many a legend and song, whose harmonious chimes rang out to us just as they pealed forth to the doughty burghers of centuries ago, whose presence we felt everywhere so vividly.

From Ghent to Belgian-French Frontier.

Returning to Ghent, an even greater mediæval capital, in the afternoon, we explored the grim recesses and terrifying dungeons of the stern Chateau des Comtes, a monumental Old World landmark to the Feudal system of the Flemish counts. And then we visited the many-chapelled St. Bavou's Cathedral, one of the finest and largest churches of Belgium, until the darkness which melted the arched heights of the nave into awe-inspiring infinity drove us back into modernism and to the preparation of our machines for the morrow.

A small room in the Grand Hotel Metropole sheltered us here for five francs ($1.00) for the "Great International exhibition of Gand," scheduled for April to October, 1913, has already boosted prices for accommodations, although few of the buildings are yet completed.

Thirty miles of level pavie led us to Brussels, the "Paris of the North," but as a splendid macadam road winding out through an extensive park invited us on, we stopped only long enough to collect our mail, before continuing thirty miles more, meeting pavie in towns only, to picturesque Namur.

Here we entered the valley of the Meuse, a strong rival of the Rhine, which we followed by romantic moonlight to quaint Dinant, putting up for the night at the Hotel Charpentier. As the valley is very steep and narrow here, the town stretches up and down the river for a mile or so and is guarded by a frowning fortress-citadel which crowns the precipitous cliffs above and dominates the entire valley.

We photographed the fort the next morning before continuing up the luxuriant valley to Givet, where we were delayed an hour in the rain at the French customs, waiting to have the chief stamp our passes and issue our "police pass," good for three months, costing one franc.

Formalities Upon Entering La Belle France.

Upon leaving Belgium, as when leaving Holland, we did not have our passes stamped as required, because this would have prevented our return without new passes, besides wasting valuable time. Unstamped, the passes would admit us any time, though, heaven knows, we have no desire to tackle Flemish roads again—not in the wet season, at least, that traveling being too dangerous.

We had our first puncture that afternoon, in Storey's back tire. It was but the forerunner of a series of mishaps that kept us three days more on the road to Paris, the fiendish French pavie, which we thought we had left behind in Belgium, causing many falls, which were the sources of most of the trouble. Later, we found this could have been avoided by sticking to the river Marne route from Meaux.

These days of exhaustive struggles were leavened by a stop at the Cathedral of Rheims—one of the finest of all Europe, and more magnificent in outside appearance and grandeur of interior—especially in its exquisite stained glass windows than Notre Dame at Paris.

OUR ARRIVAL OUTSIDE THE FORTIFICATIONS OF PARIS

We finally reached Paris, November 27, putting our machines in cold storage with the American Express Co. for 80 cents a month, and riding about town in the democratic omnibus.

Throbbing, Pulsating Paris Has Charmed Us.

We like Paris tremendously. After a two weeks visit, we have yet to see a Frenchman who isn't fully wide awake. New York or London can't compare with Paris in architectural or scenic beauty. But it is not so much in its palaces, its boulevards, or its gardens, that the chief charm of Paris lies; the secret is the vigorous, throbbing life of the French people who, through its cafes and avenues, concentrate the commercial, political and artistic expression of the whole nation. A trip through the famous Bois de Boulogne, one of the finest pieces of park system in Europe, was enjoyable, and one does not wonder why the Parisian likes his Paris. It is worth going many miles to see the life of Paris as displayed about this park.

The fact that the French are born artists is proven by a visit to the French automobile Show, or the Salon d'Automobile, held in the Grand Palais, one of the permanent buildings of the exhibition of 1900, on the Champs Elysees. Here the entire building is lighted inside and out with blended colored lights and forests of electric candles arranged in the most beautiful, but simple, designs imaginable.

But there were few motorcycles there, and most of them English makes. In fact, I have seen only four motorcycles in France, for some strange reason they being decidedly unpopular here.

The other day we went around to see the Automobile Club de France and, finding that membership would save us 10 per cent, at any of the 4,000 hotels it recommends, joined for five francs each. By accident we are living at a Touring Club hotel here, so will save our membership fee in one week. In fact, we have found it cheaper to travel on the Continent than to live in New York.

CHAPTER V
Around The World On A Motorcycle
(Fifth Installment)

A s two months must be spent in Paris for an American to grasp its full charm—to unconsciously adopt the Parisian point of view—and to feel that everything about him is right and natural, Storey and I finally realized that we were fortunate to be obliged to remain here that long.

FOLLOWING THE RIVER AFTER LEAVING PARIS.

Arriving on Thanksgiving day—celebrated in Paris by American residents only—we stored our machines in the warehouse of the American Express Company, near the Porte des Ternes, for only 80 cents a month, and allowed one of the small, lively taxis to take us, dirt and baggage, clear across the city to the far-famed Latin Quarter. The rates were only one-third those charged in New York, and this was especially surprising as gasoline, or "l'essence," costs 68 cents a gallon in Paris and but 21 cents at home.

After an hour's search, we found among the winding, narrow "rues" of this ancient "Quartier," in the midst of picturesque students of all nationalities, and close by the Luxembourg gardens and galleries, a comfortable, steam-heated, electric-lighted room in the Grand Hotel Corneille (pretentious in name only) for 100 francs, or $20, a month, plus five francs each for the "valet de chamber" who cared for the room and polished our shoes each night.

Paris a City of Past Glories and Present Splendor.

At first we took our meals at the hotel, at one franc for the Parisian breakfast of chocolate and rolls and two and one-half francs for excellent table d'hote "dejuners" and dinners, but soon found more interesting and nearly as good meals in outside restaurants, and often outside these restaurants, for the Parisian eats out of doors all winter, at half these prices. During the second month we took all our dinners at a small restaurant on Boulevard St. Michel, where a good five-course spread, including wine, totalled but 25 cents. After we had picked up a little French and learned how to order, we discovered that Paris is the cheapest of all cities for good food, and that one can live comfortably here on a total of one dollar a day.

ARC DE TRIOMPHE, PLACE ETOILE, PARIS.

Paris is recognized universally as the most beautiful city in the world, and this is largely so, I believe, because it is so purely regal. Centuries of conquerors, emperors and kings have adorned and beautified it with lavish hands. We found palaces, monuments, statues, gardens, and churches everywhere. No matter what broad avenue we looked up, some beautiful building was sure to crown its end. Where can equal stately beauty be found, to that which we met on our first morning's walk of two miles in one straight line from the Palace of the Louvre, through the Tulleries Gardens, across the Place de la Concord—of guillotine fame—and up the Champs Elysees to the Place d'Etoile, or "star," where the broad avenues converge at Napoleon's Arc de Triomphe? Or where can one view equal magnificence to that included on a ramble from the Etoile to the Trocadero and across the Seine to the foot of the "Tour Eiffel" on the Champs Mars, then on to the Hotel des Invalides and Napoleon's tomb? Or where is splendor equal to that at Versailles?

SIGN POST AND SHRINE IN CENTRAL FRANCE.

Truly, nothing short of a past like that of Paris could produce a city of such grandeur—of course nothing in America can compare with it—but this is just the point. Paris is living in its past; like London, it has had its day; unlike New York, its star is in the descendant. And this fact is what impressed me most in Paris. I longed to be back in the days of Louis XIV, and Catherine de Medici, when Paris was in flower; back when the Louvre and the Luxembourg were court centers, when their present treasures adorned the cathedrals, and the palaces of the princes and dukes for which they were prepared, and to see the royal coach grace the stately boulevards. These are the "good old days" to which the royalists (for there still is a strong party in France) look back with a sigh, while the populists recall with a shudder. And nowadays the fact that the President of this Republic is largely a figurehead was clearly proven by the lack of great excitement upon the eve of the recent election which we witnessed.

French Language "Spoken" by Tongue and Hand.

Again, try my best, I could find no excuse for Paris's existence today—except as a residential city and a place for the world's rich to come and spend money. Paris has no manufactures, no exports, and is in no wise productive—not even children, which are more scarce here than trees, even in the poorer sections. Indeed, I believe, this is why the whole French nation is on the decline—it is not sufficiently productive, except of aeroplanes, one or two of which were to be seen sailing over the city nearly every day.

The French themselves I found to be full of life, although I soon became accustomed to their vehemence.

CHAPTER VI
The Journey from Paris to Tours

Everyone uses his hands when talking, because the French language is not capable of forceful expression unaided. Soon I found myself gesticulating when endeavouring to be emphatic. For example, the French have to say "frappe du pied," or "knock with the foot," instead of the one English word "kick," and there are countless similar examples.

Influx of Foreign Motorcycles Presages Revival.

I saw only five motorcycles in Paris, and I don't wonder, for the French machines are impossible. The French are now waking up to the possibilities of American and English machines, however, and a big revival of the sport and pastime of motorcycling is predicted.

THE AUTHOR RESTS BY THE WAYSIDE.

Although the family is a live institution in Paris, the home does not seem nearly as popular as the countless restaurants where the members of the entire family often take their meals, or as the cafes where the older people spend most of their evenings, drinking coffee, listening to music, and playing games. As these cafes line the brilliantly lighted boulevards, whose broad sidewalks provide plenty of room for the tiny tables and chairs always found in front, the boulevards are the places to see the "gay" side of Paris, and we never tired of them. Between December 15 and January 15 many of them were lined with tiny stalls and booths selling candy, pictures and knickknacks, as the pointer of the crude roulette wheel that most of them employed to play upon the Frenchman's gambling instinct, would direct.

Unique Traffic Conditions and Famous Resorts.

Paris has been surrounded during its history by three different sets of fortifications. As the city grew the walls were levelled and a "bulwark" or boulevard built in its place. The present walls which surround the city proper are soon to be transformed into another boulevard—the third—some twenty miles in circumference, but an iron fence will be retained to enable the Octroi, or customs duty on wines, tobacco, food products, gasoline, etc., to be collected. The duty on "l'essance" is 2½ cents a litre, or 12 cents a gallon, but a receipt given for all essence taken out of the city in a machine's reservoir admits the entry of an equal amount free.

All the street traffic in Paris is much more dangerous than in either New York or London, being regulated at only two crossings in the entire city. I did not venture out with my Henderson until the last two weeks of my stay. But the 'busses were very rapid and cheap—three cents first class, two cents second class—and I found that the extensive subway systems were nothing of the joke I had heard them described.

DOWN THE VALLEY OF THE RIVER DORDOGNE.

In Montmartre, the Tenderloin section of Paris, we found the original Moulin Rouge, or red mill, in full action—although its propeller is now both electrically lighted and actuated; I saw the "cabaret artistique" at the subterranean café "Chat Noir," or Black Cat, and visited the "Rat Mort," Harry Thaw's favorite resort while in Paris. But none of these amusements inspired a single thrill, although the black, narrow alleys on either side caused many an involuntary shudder.

To Storey, Paris's chief attraction was its art treasures, but to me nothing could be more interesting than the scores of old churches, palaces and historical ruins, evidences of Paris's past supremacy and revolutions; monuments to Joan d'Arc, the ancient streets of Sacre Coeur, the Latin Quarter, and the gruesome catacombs.

Royal Versailles and Those Standing Armies.

But no matter where I roamed, I could not get away from the bold "Defense d'Appicher," or "post no bills" signs which are painted on practically every one of Paris's monotonous apartment and commercial buildings, or the motto "Liberte, Egalite, Fraternite," which ironically stares from every old public building and nearly every church in the city.

No motorist should fail to visit the stately palace and its wonderful gardens at Versailles, 12 miles west of Paris. If ever there was a royal habitation and a beautiful gallery, it is here; Versailles is also an important military center, and the "pretty little monkeys," or undersized, moustached men who compose a large part of the regular army, are as thick as bees in a hive. Do not ask directions from any of them, for they will pay no attention and walk away. But do not feel surprised. Remember that they are the fellows who stop the bullets and that their salary is only one cent a day. All through France, as in the British Isles and Spain, soldiers are to be found wasting time in every large town. During a dinner discussion with a German in Paris over the Balkan war, he informed me that both Russia and Austria were mobilizing their armies. "And how about Germany?" I asked. "Ah!" was his quick reply, "Germany is always mobilized." And that is one reason, I declared, why England is so afraid of her, and France, thirsting for revenge, is helpless. Germany is the dog in the manger that makes international peace nothing but a dream.

My second month in France was spent in establishing a live sales agency for the Henderson. I finally succeeded in demonstrating the merits of my machine to a large importing firm so thoroughly that I ended up by sending the export manager of the Henderson company a signed contract and order for 100 machines. The greatest handicap I had to conquer was the $60 duty on each motorcycle brought into France.

Storey Recalled and the Re-Start Made Alone.

At this point Storey was imperatively called back to America and, knowing no one to take his place, I determined to continue on "around," all alone. As the new agency was clamouring for a demonstrating machine, I sold Storey's Henderson to them. Equipped with Touring Club of France route cards clear to the Spanish border, and an indispensable Michelin guide for both France and Spain, I set out for Barcelona, 900 miles away, the following afternoon, with a heavy heart, especially as I had come to feel very much at home in Paris and to love her.

Leaving the city by the Arc de Longchampe, in the Bois de Boulogne, or municipal park, past the turf track where horse races are held all winter, I soon reached Versailles and St. Cyr, the west Point of France. After filling up with "l'essance" at 55 cents for five litres, I continued through several queer, thatch-roofed villages, not unlike those in Ireland, except for the abominable "pave" in their centers, and covered before dark 55 miles of straight, muddy roads to quaint provincial Chartes. During the last few miles the towering mass of its beautiful cathedral was my guide through the misty gloom. Here I put up at the Grand Hotel de France, because it was recommended by the Touring Club of France, and the fact that I had left Paris was brought vividly to my mind by the doubled prices—3 francs 50 centimes for dinner, instead of the accustomed 1 franc 25 centimes, and 4 francs for my room. These were the average prices charged me until I left the chateau country, 100 miles south, when room prices dropped to 2 and 3 francs. I comforted myself that night with the thought of the 10 per cent reduction I understood my Touring Club membership would secure, but the discount was refused in the morning, because I had not stated I was a T. C. member when inquiring prices. Nor have I been able to secure this discount anywhere and believe it valueless, for if I should declare I was a member of the Touring Club when entering a "recommended" hotel, prices would at once be raised to cover the discount. Membership costs but a dollar and secures unlimited touring information, so I am well pleased anyway.

Cathedral Contrasts and First View of the Loire.

As the cathedral at Chartres is famous for the wonderful, delicate stone carvings screening its altar, and the rich stained glass windows, I spent a solemn half hour here the following morning. While bare of paintings and tapestry such as enrich the cathedrals of Brughes and Ghent, the stately beauty of the vaulted Gothic interior would inspire a feeling of worship in the most hardened heart. If America was equipped with similar "Houses of God" I feel that our church institutions would be more popular and influential. One thing that surprised me was that a small town had such a magnificent cathedral, almost as large as Notre Dame at Paris, which latter disappointed me because it was excelled by the peerless edifice at Rheims.

THE CHATEAU AT CHENONCEAUX, THE BEAUTIFUL.

Sixty-three miles straight south that afternoon, through many a staring town and past many minor chateaux, brought me to Blois at 3:45. Securing shelter in the Hotel du Chateau, I stabled the machine in one of the old wine vaults under the chateau itself, climbed the lofty terrace from which it dominates the town, and gloried in my first view of the romantic Loire—the Rhine of France—which wound its way for many leagues to the north and south. Here I was at last, at the very front door of history!

FRONT OF THE FAMOUS TOURS CATHEDRAL.

'Mid Scenes of Intrigue and Plot, Centuries Old.

Finding it too late to enter the chateau, I explored the ancient town below and was delighted to discover one of the same narrow streets I used to read about, where the upper stories of the opposite buildings, overhanging the pavement, seem almost to touch each other.

I arose early enough the next morning to get my machine in shape for a hard day's run, and 9 o'clock found me clanging at the portal of the varied mass of buildings, built between 1200 and 1635, composing the chateau itself. As it was in the off season, I had this residence of kings, queens, princes and dukes of royal blood all to myself, except for my guide, who seemed much pleased with himself when he could utter a word in English. Yet here I was oppressed with the same feeling I experienced in Paris. O, if the last 400 years could be for a moment banished! This desire became somewhat subdued after I had climbed the beautiful spiral staircase, for which Blois is noted, seen the spot where the Duke of Guise was murdered by order of Henry III. in 1558 (merely because he wanted to be King), inspected the secret cabinets where Catherine de Medici kept her poisons, and shuddered in the dungeon where Cardinal Lorraine was assassinated. Nor did a terrific hailstorm which suddenly swept through the valley, shrieking in the great chimneys and secret staircases of the darkened halls, and filling the heavy air with weird sighs and groans, tend to cheer things up, with their echoes of the tragedies of the past.

Nearly all the rooms were long and low, and bare, except for the elaborate coats of arms which covered the walls and timbered ceilings with Charles XII.'s salamanders and his queen, Anne of Brittany's, ermine, and the gaudy restored fireplaces. Originally, tapestry hung on the walls and divided each room into an apartment of three chambers, but this had disappeared, except in the great council hall.

After spending another absorbing hour in the museum, or picture gallery, of the chateau, the rain ceased and, with only half a day ahead of me, I started out to visit four other chateaux and cover 66 miles before night. I succeeded and saw many smaller fairy castles as well. So plentiful were they, in fact, I concluded that lovely Touraine, or Loraine as it is often called, must once have been a veritable enchanted land.

Ideals and Ambitions, Prospected and Realized.

VIEW OF THE QUEER HILLSIDE AT LACOVE.

As I had planned my route to include some of the more noted of the scores of these feudal strongholds with the least possible detour, seven miles of muddy road led me to Cheverny, a very fine specimen of unfortified mansion, built in 1630, but not nearly so interesting as the majestic Chateau of Chaumont, which I managed to find after following a rocky lumber road for 12 miles through the forest of Russy, where Francis I. used to hunt.

Chaumont, in location, architecture, and size, is the castle of my childhood dreams in reality. Of all, it is my favourite chateau. Sometime I hope to buy it, and even now it is owned and inhabited, as is Cheverny, Chenonceaux and a dozen other renowned castles, by an American millionaire. Built during the reign of Louis XIII., its architecture—towers, gables and dungeons—are a mixture of late Gothic and early Renaissance, strikingly appropriate for its surroundings, whether viewed from the valley of the Loire, which it commands, or from the extensive gardens at its rear. In 1500 Catherine de Medici, Queen of Henry II., bought the chateau from the Chaumont family and compelled Diana of Poitiers, the fair favourite of her husband, to exchange for it the Chateau of Chenonceaux, a more grand but less romantic castle, which I found bridging the Cher, 20 miles to the southwest.

At Chenonceaux, as at Chaumont, and all other isolated chateaux, the concierge at the entrance gate prevented me from bringing my Henderson near enough to photograph it and the chateau together. Placing the Ansco on my luggage, however, I snapped the splendid approach to this "turreted architectural gem" and later bottled up a brook-side view of the palace as the light of the setting sun painted the rippling river in true water colors.

One franc at the drawbridge (still raised every night) secured entrance to the lower floors, for the "Terrys," the American owners, were "wintering in Cuba," and a comparison of the carefully restored interior with the widely different one at Blois, was most interesting. The extravagant tastes and splendour of both Diana and Catherine, who added the two-storied gallery crossing the river to the original building, was plainly evident. Taking it altogether—the entrancing valley, the quiet river, the great park—and the beautiful castle—the pure liveliness of this fairy spot was indescribable.

Queen Catherine Inseparably Linked With History.

At four o'clock, with still 37 miles to go, I set out on good departmental roads, winding over hill and valley, for Amboise— "one of the finest historical monuments in France" dominating, like Blois, the right bank of the Loire. An entire book easily could be written describing the history that has been made behind these walls. Here it was that the horrible massacre of the Huguenots in the religious wars—the prelude of the greater slaughter in Paris on the eve of St. Bartholomew, took place in 1560, instigated by the demon-queen Catherine, who witnessed the 1200 deaths from her apartment above. Indeed, like the "defense d'afficher" signs of Paris, Catherine de Medici seems to be inseparable from the history of practically every chateau and chapter record of that section.

Originally built by the Romans, Amboise was ruined by the Normans in the Ninth Century and rebuilt by the Counts of Anjou toward the end of the Tenth Century. During the Fifteenth and Sixteenth centuries it was the favourite residence of the French kings.

One of the most prominent features of the castle is the Tour de Minimes, a huge round tower containing a wonderful inclined roadway so wide and large that a coach and four and a cavalcade of troops used to get up by it. I wanted to try the ascent with the Henderson, but the guard hadn't a drop of sporting blood in him.

A twilight ride of 15 miles down the silent Loire brought me to Tours, where the crowd which gathered about my machine was so great that traffic was completely stalled, and only after several gendarmes had forced through an alleyway was I able to proceed past the gauntlet of staring eyes to my hotel.

CHAPTER VII
Out of France and Into Sunny Spain

Being the Seventh Installment of C. S. Clancy's Narrative
of His Journey Around the World on a Motorcycle

If ever the term "picturesque" can be aptly applied to a locality, it exactly describes the delightful foothills of the Pyrenees. Evidently a land of great fertility, miles of vineyards basked in the cordial sun and lazy, dark-skinned peasants were pruning the winter's growth of sprouts, and plowing crosswise the deep, brown furrows of last season. Time means next to nothing here—in fact, all through this country they close the gates at the railroad crossings at five minutes before the train is due, and as the train is seldom on time, the nature of a people who will put up with this regulation is apparent. I arrived at one of these gates one minute after it had been closed, and actually had to fight the woman guard before I could push my machine through the pedestrian gates and get across. At last she gave up and burst into tears, running off with a mixture of cries in which "Mon Dieu! Mon Dieu!" played an important part. The train might have come along sometime, but though I followed the track for miles I never saw it.

73

ROAD BESIDE THE DORDAGNE RIVER.

In the Valley of the Aude.

Here it was that I said good-bye to mud, as I had to pavie in the north, and exchanged for it the dust of a two months' stretch without rain. After following an undulating road a few miles, I entered the valley of the Aude, which led on in such rapidly ascending turns that the tiny railroad on the opposite bank became utterly demoralized and frequently had to hide its head in long, dark tunnels. Endeavoring to make time, I slid around these turns with less caution than was necessary and nearly came to grief upon a string of those two-wheeled carts of hay, drawn by a line of three or four gaunt horses, which, together with similar caravans of enormous casks of wine, form the principal commerce of this district. The first driver perched on one side of the broad shafts behind the rear horse was asleep, of course, as were the drivers of all the carts that followed, and as was the driver of nearly all the carts I met in Spain. Nothing saved me but the broad ditch on the right and the agility of the dog that was occupying it.

ENTRANCE TO CHENONCEAUX CHATEAU

Out On a High Plateau.

Passing through Limoux and Quillan, the massive peaks towered nearer and nearer and higher and higher ahead of me, until the narrowing valley changed into a veritable gorge of ragged gray rock, on one side of which, hewn out of solid rock, the road wound for miles in and out of tunnels and on the edge of dizzy cliffs. My! What force must have existed to rend this terrible canyon in the earth's crust—for plainly it existed long before the river, now dwindled to a roaring stream, had rolled its first pebble. Higher and higher the road climbed—so well graded was it that comparatively little power was required—until the gorge suddenly widened and I found myself upon a high plateau at the very foot of the canopied pinnacles which had guided me from beneath.

From Cold Heights to a Warm Valley.

Now I could begin to realize what a mountain that lifted its head 10,000 feet above the sea was like! The grandeur of the scene was overpowering. Yes, there must be a God—a God who seemed much more real at that time than pigmy brother man crawling below.

IN THE SOUTH OF FRANCE HIGHLANDS

Wow! How cold it was! The chill wind now began to corral the black clouds that hovered on the lower peaks so actively that I was glad to speed down away from the maze of these savage giants to the inviting valley of the Agly stretching away to the east. Here the mountain peasants all wear curious red caps not unlike the "bonnet rouge" of Revolutionary days, broad red sashes about their waists, and baggy corduroy trousers of dark browns and greens. The teamsters vary this fashion with "barets" of blue, and bedeck their horses with red and drab tassels hanging to the curious three-pronged devil's horns of their breast plates. Here also numerous groves of almond trees—which I first thought were peach—put in appearance, and everywhere the red-roofed cottages dotting the landscape put the finishing touches to this colourful land. Often the horizon line would display a ruined castle hewn out of the solid rock of the mountain, fascinating me with images of its forgotten past.

REPAIRING A TIRE IN THE PYRENEES.

My First Spanish Carnival.

For 20 miles more—from St. Paul to Estagel—the mountains flanked the splendid road, and as I took my last peep backward the golden disk of the setting sun, lending a mellow glow to the haze of blue, harmonized the whole color scheme into a vision that will never be forgotten.

MONTE DE BELLIVER AND CHATEAU.

At Perpignan, only eight miles from the Mediterranean, and the first place where I had to put my machine into a garage for the night, a carnival was in progress, and the brilliantly lighted streets and "rambla," another Spanish institution, were thronged with masked and costumed revellers and crowded with oddly-dressed peasants. But even the fireworks, due at 11 o'clock, could not tempt me from my downy couch and the preparation for the morrow's advance to Spain.

The excitement in the mountain villages through which I passed upon my actual crossing of the Pyrenees the next morning was even more humorous than in the mountains of Lot. One little maid, fearing for the safety of her lively pig, grabbed him by an ear and hauled him, loudly squealing, into the ditch. Meanwhile a tiny donkey, loaded down with two huge baskets bulging on each side and one man in the middle, executed a most graceful waltz—only, instead of embracing, his partner sat on him; very much so! Time and again I would meet large flocks of sheep and goats whose shepherd, leading them Bible fashion, would almost invariably take them far into the neighboring field—very needlessly though, for I had no desire to take a wheel off from any of them. Mules as well as donkeys are very popular as steeds in the mountains, and many passes are impossible for the numerous awkward carts.

CATHEDRAL ON MEDITERRANEAN
ISLAND OFF COAST OF SPAIN.

Held Up at the Spanish Frontier.

Another rugged valley led me up the divide to le Pertus, where the French customs officials insisted upon stamping my travelling pass—the thing I had avoided when leaving Holland and Belgium—and a little further on a villainous Spaniard, bedecked in the most dressy of uniforms, blocked my entrance into sunny Spain. Without even changing the leer on his lips, he made me open my luggage and then disappeared with my papers into a neighboring office, while a group of queerly-dressed Spanish soldiers pointed with evil eyes to the Stars and Stripes sailing at my masthead, muttering under their breath "Estados Unidos!"

Soon the chief of the frontier himself came out to announce that my pass was no good in Spain, but though I easily guessed the meaning of this cigarette-fiend—though gentleman he was—it was not until a young chap who could speak French arrived on the scene was I able to ascertain just how much duty the "Aduanda" planned to hold me up for. The weight of the machine was the basis worked on, and the 272 pesetas required for the 90 kilograms boiled down to $54.40 in American money—plus $1.00 for the "formalite." Gold was demanded as essential, but as this was not forthcoming, French paper was finally accepted—change being rendered in Spanish paper and silver, which is about 3 per cent below par. An elaborate document was then prepared, stamped, and signed with many a flourish, in return for which I was told my deposit would be immediately refunded upon leaving the country, but if I lost the paper the money was lost! I was also informed it was customary to tip the inspector, so after bestowing six cents upon this veritable brigand, I started off for Barcelona, 120 miles away.

I had not proceeded half a mile, however, before another officer stopped me and demanded my new papers, which proved satisfactory. A quarter of a mile further on a second individual in plain clothes (probably a police officer) again brought me to a sudden halt. Truly the Spanish were taking no chances, I thought, but the procedure was getting decidedly tiresome and I wondered how long it would last. But he proved to be the last blockade I was to encounter until I left Spain—and then! —but that comes later.

I had expected poor roads in Spain, and was not happily disappointed. To all those who are planning to motorcycle in Spain let me give this one word of advice—don't! Occasionally

I would meet a stretch of smooth surface, but for the most part the roads were so full of holes, and water-breaks, and fords, that there was no fun in it. Over 15 miles an hour is impossible except to a well sprung automobile—and one might just as well stay in France. In fact, except near the Pyrenees, along the Mediterranean, and in Barcelona, Spain is not especially interesting—although the climate is truly delightful and the mountains magnificent.

Motor Trouble Halts Trip.

But I was not destined to reach Barcelona that night for a bad knock developed in my motor upon entering the ancient town of Figueras, and I determined to investigate. Here it was that my absolute ignorance of Spanish was rammed home most strongly. Asking for a garage, I was guided to a hotel instead, with half the town at my heels. A Frenchman who finally came to my rescue informed me that there was no garage in town, and led me to a bicycle shop, where I was able to shut the door on the crowd and inspect my cylinders. Finding that a mass of carbon collected from the poor oil I had been forced to buy at Loches had caused pre-ignition and broken one of my crank shaft bearings, I decided to continue by train to Barcelona, where my spare parts sent on ahead in my trunk would provide the new pieces. But the latter of the two daily trains had already gone, so my first night in Spain was spent in the Hotel de Paris of this balconied town, where the waiter brought me a bottle of wine when I asked for the bill.

Indeed, I did not reach Barcelona until the following night, the wretched hencoop train taking seven hours to cover the 100 miles, so I had plenty of time to observe Spanish customs and character. On the average, the Spanish were more attractive to me than the French both in looks and temperament. Except for the

Catalans, who inhabit the Pyrenee district and have an entirely distinct native language, the Spanish seemed very strongly Latin, even more gay than the Italians in nature. To anyone who has studied Latin, Spanish is very easy to learn, many of the words being adapted without change, and being pronounced as they are spelled, but at first I was obliged to fall back upon my slight knowledge of French when making my requirements known.

As it almost never rains here, the air is wonderfully clear and the people very dark in skin. Like the Arabs, they also wear an habitual squint, acquired from constantly winking at the sun. They seemed more languid than the French and to value time very cheaply. They also found it as hard to keep warm as I to keep cool, and bundled their mouths and throats with great mufflers in spite of the hot sun. In the train iron tanks of hot water were provided to keep their feet warm, and the nights get cold enough for frosts.

Unlike France, every fertile foot of land in Spain is under active cultivation. This is so intensive that the steep hillsides are terraced with stone walls to form tiny gardens. Olive groves are plentiful as well as the universal dwarf grape vine, and patient oxen are often to be seen dragging old-fashioned plows across the fields, for in many respects Spain is a century behind the times. It was in Figueras that I saw my first palm tree—a magnificent specimen of the date variety, 500 years old, and to-day I saw my first orange tree, in full fruit!

Most of the rivers we crossed were dry, and not a single lake was visible on the entire ride. Water is so scarce that irrigation has long been necessary, windmills being sometimes used to pump well water into an elevated reservoir, but more often the water is raised and carried by hand. Today also I saw my first "castle in Spain" and scores of them, for they are even more numerous than the chateaux of Loraine, one dominating nearly every commanding hill in the district. Surely this land has seen stirring times!

The architecture of the towns and plastered farm villas was monotonously flat and square, but the colors were decidedly original—pink being most in vogue. In fact, the Spanish seem as fond of brilliant colors as they are of jewelry—and this is being emphatic! As Spain is very mountainous snow crested peaks (the sunny side of which melt during the day and freeze up each night) were visible until within 50 miles of Barcelona. And the laughing children, on the train, playing in towns, everywhere, were most refreshing.

CHAPTER VIII
Clancy Quits Spain for Algeria

Being the Eighth Installment of The Story of His Tour Around the World on a Motorcycle

Barcelona might well be called the city of broad streets, as the main avenues are twice the width of upper Broadway, New York City. Alighting from the jolting train, much more weary than if I had motorcycled the 100 miles, the proprietor of a "pension" where everything was "tout compris" for five pesetas, or a dollar a day, decoyed me to his den and surprised me with a two-room apartment, including a balcony overlooking the Paseo de Colon, a long, straight avenue lined with two rows of splendid palms, bordering the harbour front. The dinner, too, was better than I expected from the general uncleanliness of the place, and differed from a French meal only in the details that each portion was larger and rarely hot enough. But my chief objection was the monotony of taste, by which I correctly deduced that everything was cooked in the same pot of olive oil, which entirely replaces butter and lard in Spanish kitchens. The fact that the Spanish are a cleanly people is shown by the entire absence of flies. One senora told me that flies would starve there because even the hard dirt streets are swept and sprinkled with water every night.

In Spain nearly every window is a door opening in its center onto a tiny balcony. The view of the brilliantly lighted Ramblas from mine that evening drew me out to mix with the fascinating throng. Here between two rows of enormous white button-ball or platinum trees, a splendid promenade varying from 60 to 100 feet in breadth occupied the center of a Paseo for its entire length of a full mile. The roadway bordered each side and then came the regular sidewalks, but these were deserted for the crowded Rambla—resembling the boardwalk at Atlantic City more than anything else.

MARKET PLACE IN FIGUERAS.

TYPICAL SCENE IN ONE OF BARCELONA'S WIDE STREETS.

Everyone seemed to be promenading—and to be happy! All casts and all colors jostled each other. Mountain peasants with their queer red caps perched jauntily on one side, weather beaten sailors, smart looking soldiers, entreating flower girls, the prosperous merchant with his whole family, the soft brown eyed, black haired senorita—who would inspire a serenade from almost any lad of spirit—and the dainty, white-gloved grandame—who reminded me strongly of a new doll—and delicately watched over them all. Constantly I would be startled with the strange "ptsst" or snake-like hiss with which friends called to each other, or a waiter's attention was secured, the whistle never being used here.

Gaiety of Barcelona.

Many of the shops were open, but the soda fountains on the Ramblas themselves—the first I have found in Europe—were the greatest attraction for me until I found that the Spanish do not know how to mix syrup drinks. Numerous great squares of palm and other tropical trees strengthened my feeling that there is an abundance of breathing space in Barcelona, and lined as they were with cafes teeming with laughing people, made me sure that Paris is no more comfortable and not half so gay.

The following morning the sun rising out of the harbour opposite my window, inspired a resolve to get a bird's-eye view of this historic sea, and as my diary was written "on the spot" I will quote from it verbatim: "A zealous sentry has just ejected me from the old Spanish castle of Montjuich, which crowns the mountain to the right of the beautiful city of Barcelona, so now I am resting in the shade of this important fortress, revelling in the azure blueness of the placid Mediterranean stretching away to the southern horizon, the colourful city laid out at my left, and the crescent of terraced mountains that overlook the city to the north. Bells are ringing continuously, and snatches of opera from a light-hearted peasant or a gay hand organ mix with the shrill whistles of the busy harbor at my feet. Barcelona is noted for its extensive commerce, and ships of all flags and varied gargos lie harmoniously together in the wide lagoons back of the extensive sea walls which shelter the entire city from the fury of a storm. Just beyond a long quay loaded with olive oil, wine, and tropical fruits, I can plainly discern the long, white steamer that is soon to take me to the Baleric Isles and then on to Algiers. Even now two big freighters are leaving the harbour for East Indian ports."

Balmy Weather in Spain.

Although early in February, the climate here is like June in New England. Cactus plants line the road leading down to the city, and in the little gardens on each side almond trees are in blossom and orange trees in fruit. The Barcelonians regard it as winter, nevertheless, and as they go about wrapped in fur coats and mufflers the contrast between this temperature and that of actual summer must be very marked.

Some persons say Barcelona is more beautiful than Paris, but surely not in its architecture, for my bird's-eye view shows only a tiresome mass of white and buff plastered buildings, with flat roofs land scarcely a red tile to brighten the picture. All are about the same height and character, many look as if they would crumble if you stuck your finger into them, and although Barcelona is nearly as large as Madrid, and the second city in the land, the skyline is rarely relieved by a church or public building, and then it has no great interest. A notable exception is the case of the Arena, where bull fights are held each spring, a veritable modern coliseum and monument to the influence of "barbaric Rome."

Trunk Causes Annoying Delay.

Returning to the city, I found that my trunk had not arrived, being held for customs examination at the railroad frontier. After endless waiting and interviewing of scores of useless officials, I found it would be necessary to send my key to the frontier—and then to wait! Although I could not see why they could not examine the trunk in Barcelona as well as on the frontier, I entrusted my key to a cut-throat officer—and waited!

But waiting was not conducive to the speedy repair of my machine, so I took the five o'clock train back to Figueras the next morning, resolved to save time by having the bearing made there. The train was packed with peasants returning from their Sunday holiday in the city, and my only comfort was the music of two original troubadours who alternately played an accordion and accompanied each other on a banjo, singing bits of opera the whole dreary way.

Repair Costs Run High.

I lost out again, however, for a rod had first to be cast from phosphor bronze, then turned and bored and halved accurately and fitted, so by the time the job was complete (including the straightening of the front fork) three days and $25 had been used up by the careful but exasperatingly slow mechanic and his two ornamental assistants.

With only 24 hours to get myself and baggage aboard the weekly boat for Africa, I set out at 5:30 that afternoon over the unknown road to Barcelona, and the fact that I covered 60 miles before the new moon went down at 9 o'clock, is little short of a miracle. The wretched roads shook me to pulp, and the fact that I could not see the holes and stones added to my misery. When I passed through Gerona with its miles of narrow, crooked streets at seven o'clock, I stopped to buy a huge roll of bread to pack my churned insides so they would not rattle quite so loud.

From there on I did not see a single living person or pass a house for 20 miles. Wow! How lonely it was—and I had left my Savage automatic in Barcelona! Getting caught in a rut, a nasty fall smashed my lamp, and a little further on another almost broke my leg, but the fords were my worst trouble! Being the watershed for the whole range of mountains to the north, these plains were furrowed with countless streams and a number of respectable rivers, even in this dry season. Only one river on the whole route boasted a bridge, and after a hard rain the road would have been absolutely impossible. What shook my nerve was to have the shadow at the bottom of a sharp descent suddenly turn into a 40-foot river of hidden depth. Usually I was able to stop on the brink, and then walking on an occasional flagstone, laboriously push the machine through the muddy streams, none of which proved over two feet in depth. After a while I got so I didn't care—philosophically reflecting that one must die sometime and to die with one's boots on is very noble; so I rushed all the fords that came later, and surprised myself each time by reaching the other side alive. My dear old Henderson even seemed to enjoy the excitement.

Grocery Store Provides Shelter.

But with no moon and no lamp, I had to quit at last, and the "Fonda" of the crumbling village of Tordera raised its shutter to shelter my machine in the grocery store that formed the main entrance, and provide a place to lay my head. Although I hadn't seen a soul in the place except the man who guided me to that imitation hotel, before I had finished my supper of coffee and toast, an eager crowd had gathered about the table and blocked the doorway, its members watching every movement of my jaws with the same expression as if I had been a mermaid from Mars. Finally a chap who thought he could talk French elbowed his way in and did his best to learn all my business and family history, but after vainly endeavouring to buy them all a drink, I succeeded in slipping away to my windowless room.

Gasolene Comes High in Spain.

Gasolene prices broke the record here the next morning at 20 cents a litre (or 90 cents a gallon), so I said, "I'll take only three, please," which were more than sufficient to carry me the 40 miles along the balmy, picturesque seacoast, the road winding on the face of great cliffs for many leagues, to Barcelona, at last!

My trunk and key arrived that very morning also, so after buying my boat ticket and enjoying a good meal, I thought my troubles for the day were over. Not a bit of it, though, for when I called at the Aduanda for my customs deposit at 1:30, and as the "officials" were taking their three-hour noon holiday, again at 3:00 o'clock, I found that the refund department operated only from 8:30 until 1:00 P. M. and that no money was forthcoming until tomorrow; also, that I would have to get the signature of the captain of the ship I sailed on, upon my document, to show that the machine had actually been embarked, before the refund would be given. (I had to dig all this out of a broadside of Spanish.) No amount of entreaty would make them open the office for me—though it could all have been over in a few minutes—and not wishing to forfeit $55.00 and my ticket, or wait a week for the next boat—especially as I had nearly broken my neck to catch this one—I was "up a tree" indeed.

Tourist Agency to the Rescue.

With only two hours before sailing time I repaired to the haven of refuge of all Americans in foreign cities—Thos. Cook & Sons' office—and there had my difficulty solved (but for the day only) with the information that as the Baleric Islands belong to Spain I would not leave the country until the boat departed from Palma for Algiers the following night. With great rejoicing and hallelujas in my heart, I finally got the machine and all my possessions on the boat, and for the first time in seeming ages, relaxed!

CHAPTER IX
Among the Arabs of Northern Africa

The Ninth Installment of Carl Stearns Clancy's
Narrative of His Journey, Now in Progress
Around the World on a Motorcycle

The beautiful city and bay of Palma greeted my eyes the following morning, and after moving into a sister steamer, I set out to explore the town, resolving to be bright and early at the custom house. The captain of the new boat refused to sign the receipt for my machine, stating that the operating company's office would have to do it, so after locating that establishment also and finding them both closed, I indulged in a breakfast of eggs and coffee on the broad veranda of the Hotel Alhambra for one peseta, or 19 cents, having to draw a picture of a hen and two specimens of her fruit before my order was understood.

Custom House Delays.

At 9:00 o'clock at the custom house I was again plunged into the deepest gloom, for—insanity of insanities! —I was informed in unflinching terms that my deposit could not be refunded that day, nor for several days, not only because they did not have $55 in the place, but because the regulations required that my identical deposit must be refunded, and that the frontier would have to be written for it! Can you imagine what a hot-headed Spaniard who had entered a motor car at New York and wanted to sail with it from San Francisco, would say if told that he would have to wait until New York could be written to for his deposit? Well that's what I felt like saying then—only worse. I was stunned by the idiot way in which the Spanish government does business. In this condition I wandered aimlessly back to the steamboat office and laid my case before an imposing official there. Being too busy to be charitable just then (reading his newspaper), he told me to return at 11:00 o'clock; so I sought consolation in the great cathedral that dominates the city.

A Form of Spanish Graft.

The Spanish cathedrals are very different from the French, both in architecture, which is more a combined Roman and Byzantine than Gothic, and in interior decoration. Here the altars are very large and gaudy, being plastered with gold and mosaics. Even the altars of the smaller chapels surpass in splendour the main altar of a French church. The large "sinner's room" is another unique institution; and outside bells distinguish the smaller churches. The stained glass windows are on the same order as the altars, of clashing colors and awkward design. Although an elaborate service was in progress when I entered, the cathedral at Palma was as empty of people as a huge barn, which its interior resembled. In fact, there were not more than 20 chairs in the place, so I gathered that this house of worship was habitually empty—a self-sufficient institution, so to speak. The organ was good, so I rested here and meditated upon my sins and some few of those of the Aduanda.

The appointed hour found me back at the steamboat office, and after a further half-hour's wait the official told me that the transportation company would refund my deposit for me—less the $4 the government demanded for no visible reason at all, except pure graft. Again my sorrows were reversed! It took two hours more to prepare and sign the necessary transfer papers, and then I actually secured $50 of my original $55. Oh, if that villain at the frontier had only been a little more explicit!

As the Algerian boat did not sail until 5:00 o'clock, or 17 o'clock as they call it here, I spent two hours exploring the city and the great castle that once guarded the bay from a neighboring height. And yet my troubles were not over, for a strong northeast wind provided a beautiful trough for the little Glasgow-built boat to wallow in during the entire 14 hours of the crossing, and for the first time I was really seasick. I wished a hundred times I had never survived that night ride in Spain! Altogether, it cost $7 for my second-class berth, $2 for the machine, and a good dinner to get me across the Mediterranean.

Demands of the Arab Chief.

One who does not take a motor into Algiers misses half the opportunities the colony offers for exciting adventure. The harbour of the city is so shallow that even the small steamer from Palma could not tie up along the quay, so the passengers and all the cargo—including my worthy Henderson—had to be embarked in small boats and big barges plying from the anchorage to the shore. Scores of swarthy, bare-legged Arab boatmen swarmed about the foot of the companion stairs, and overran the boat in search of luggage, so it was an easy matter to get everything ashore at the custom house.

BAY AND CITY OF PALMA ON THE ISLAND OF MAJORCA.

The aid of no less than seven of these dirty savages, who insisted upon doing everything I wanted to do myself, was forced upon me, in spite of emphatic protests. But all went well until I tried to pay the Arab chief, or foreman who employed all the boatmen, for their services. This magnificent individual—a splendid, fez-capped specimen about six and a half feet high—was politeness itself and accompanied me to the train line, where he answered my inquiry of his charge with, "Oh, monsieur, what you like!" Thinking him a really decent Arab after all, I concluded to be generous, and tendered him five francs, or $1.00. Did he take it? I guess not! —not even would he touch it. Promptly he found he had a price—one pound, or $5.00, no less. I was so surprised that I laughed in his face, whereupon he graciously came down to 20 francs, or $4.00. "What!" said I, "40 francs for my two trips from a boat 300 yards from the wharf, and for carrying my motorcycle on a barge loaded with luggage the same distance? No! Five francs is all you will get, and you ought to be thankful for that."

TYPICAL STREET SCENE IN PALMA.

His Friends Endorse His Claim.

Instantly all his former courtesy changed to righteous indignation. His eyes glared fire and my complete annihilation seemed imminent. Over and over again he roaringly enumerated all the details of his services few of which I had asked of him, and several imaginary ones, laying much emphasis on the Henderson, which he insisted upon calling "the auto," and always ending up with his demand for 20 francs.

Finding me still calm and firm in my refusal, he called several of his employees and friends—related to each and all of them the whole story (from his point of view) and demanded their opinion, which invariably seconded his own. Soon I was the amused center of a crowd of yelling Arabs, and also the center of interest of all the passers-by, except the native policemen, who evinced none whatever in the proceedings.

Outwitting the Enemy.

At last I got sick of the delay, and as the Arab would not touch my money, I pocketed it and boarded the car for my hotel. But the enraged chief was not thus to be baffled; he jumped on the same tram, righteously exclaiming that if I "would not pay for his work my hotel proprietor would." But as my host spoke excellent English, I was able to explain the situation clearly and gained my first supporter. Instead of paying the Arab more, he told him to take my dollar or he would kick him out. Foiled again, the lusty savage flung out of the house with the parting threat, "I'll see you on the wharf in the morning."

The clearance of my machine through the Algerian customs, where it was held during the night, compelled my presence on the dock the next A. M., but not wishing to enter this den of thieves alone again, I sought aid from the Algerian "succursal," or branch house of the Parisian firm who took the Henderson agency for France and Northern Africa. Here I was most cordially received and supplied with a brave mechanic guard, who sumptuously drove me down to the "Douane" in a Ford touring car.

As I expected, "les Arabe" operated a regular "system," combining for all I knew all the villainous traits of both the Black Handers of Italy and the Yogi of India. One heathen had called at my hotel during my absence at breakfast, making a vain attempt to secure my custom's papers, and when my interpreter and I reached the dock the gang's sentry was waiting to hiss the signal of my arrival. The "chief" appeared immediately, but kept a strategic distance until the Henderson had been ransomed from the clutches of the Douane. This latter operation proved as simple as my entry into Spain had been complicated, for my travelling pass proved entirely satisfactory (after several books of rules had been arduously consulted by the careful officials), and in an hour more the machine was delivered in exchange for only three cents, for a receipt stamp—intact, except for the theft of my tiny Stars and Stripes, which had safely overcome all the dangers of France and Spain.

As the officials of both boats from Barcelona and Palma had forgotten to order me to drain my gas tank, I still had half a gallon of power juice, and soon my motor was humming merrily. But when I started to mount the Arabs crowded around and tried to prevent me—but not quickly enough. The same arguments of yesterday soon waxed even hotter than my motor, which I shut off after it was nicely warmed up (would that the Arabs were so docile!). With the mechanic in the thickest of the fight, the center of attention shifted to him. So, taking advantage of an open space, I pushed my machine suddenly forward when straddling it, pulled in my clutch, the motor started, and before the villainous crowd knew what was doing I was away up the hill in the town, with the mechanic hard after me in the Ford.

The garage was clear at the south end of the city—and there were several others I might have gone to—but not ten minutes after my arrival the Arab chief had found me and taken up sentry duty at the only entrance. I was a prisoner! At last I resolved to end his tyranny and went out to the final fray. I got him down to 15, then to 10 francs, where he stuck as firmly as I stuck to my five-franc limit. All the garage force and several hotel interpreters were drawn into the litigation, but as a matter of principle I refused to give in to the exorbitant charge. Eventually it was decided to lay the case before the commissioners of police—one native and one French—who at last decided in my favour at eight francs—some difference between the 25 first demanded! Again I breathed freely, and heeded not my adversary's threats of revenge at the hour of sailing—for, unknown to him, I was to sail from Tunis, not Algiers.

Impressions of Algiers.

Aside from its Arab quarter, Algiers is an attractive city, like Tours, a miniature Paris, with its big cafes, modern apartment houses and smart branch shops of Parisian merchants. Built on the face of a hill, its European section borders the harbour front, while the Arabs—the name generally applied to all the mixed native population—infest the narrow, staired streets of the higher slopes. To these former lords of the land is now consigned all the dirty work—ditch digging, transporting local freight, selling papers, and operations similar to those performed by negroes and immigrants in America. But most of these squalid, turbaned creatures—including the small remaining landed aristocracy— spend their time sitting in doorways or by the roadside, doing absolutely nothing but smoke cigarettes the whole day long. Indeed, it was a constant wonder to me how thousands of these natives lived. Apparent poverty reigned universal, yet everyone seemed well fed, including the dried up, woe begone, barefooted old women, who hobbled about the streets in scores, and especially the numerous ragged children who supported their lazy parents by brazen begging.

How the Arabs Dress.

Stockings or socks are almost unknown in the Arab quarter, and the small percentage boasting shoes or slippers were apparently supplied them from the refuse pail of the European section. The Arab costume most in vogue seemed to consist of two sheets and one rough towel, one sheet wound about the torso of the body from top to bottom, the other wrapped about sideways, while the bath towel, usually colored partly red, was around the closely shaven head just above the protruding ears to form a large turban. This headdress was exchanged by some tribes for a small red fez-cap, shaped like an inverted flower pot and adorned by a long, black tassel. Many of the women wore long, heavy veils from their eyes downward, and I thought it would be a splendid idea if most of the men would adopt the same custom.

PRIMITIVE METHOD EMPLOYED FOR
IRRIGATING THE LAND IN ALGIERS.

In the "Garden of Allah."

Aside from the magnificent white public buildings recently built by the French along the lines of Mohammedan mosques or in Moorish architecture, the most ornamental objects of the city were the flashy French soldiers in costumes widely varying, according to their regiment, to be seen everywhere. The "Zouaves," huge, square-bearded fellows—both French and native soldiers were most brilliant in their long, red bloomers and short, black jackets, with their white capes lined with crimson thrown carelessly back over one shoulder. The cavalry men were also most attractive in their shiny, spurred boots, short, red, peg-topped trousers with a high "princess" waist, tight blue jacket, and natty Russian cap.

But it was not until late at night that I fully awoke to the fact that I was actually in the capital of "The Garden of Allah," for then the long, fearsome wail of the winter wind as it swept around the corner of my room, making me shudder at its ominous loneliness, forced upon me the sudden realization that the weird cry of the desert windstorm reproduced in that popular play, had not been exaggerated.

Living was not so cheap here as at Paris, meals costing from 35 to 60 cents each at ordinary restaurants, and my room 70 cents a day at the modern Hotel Regina. Another extra dollar went to pay the American consul for his minute's courtesy of "vising" my passport, an operation insisted upon by the French postal authorities before they would deliver a registered letter from New York.

I spent a week in Algiers, working night and day upon the written description of my adventures between Paris and Barcelona; and then, with only five days to catch the boat from Tunis (650 miles away) to Naples, I set out in a hard rain for the "interior" of this Mohammedan land, still wrapped in the veil of mystery. Foreboding it was to me, also, for inquiries as to whether it was safe to travel alone through these territories had been answered by some in the affirmative. Still, with my "10-shot-quick Savage" in my hip pocket, a big, new horn, the Michelin guide for my pilot, and two road maps, I resolved to take the chance.

Through an African Storm.

Africa—how strange my presence seemed! —did not live up to its reputation as "the land of never-fading azure," for the rain which I first welcomed for laying the dust had continued during the last three days before my departure, turning the dust into deep, slippery mud. A sharp hailstorm at the moment of leaving prevented the taking of a photo of my start, but did not chill or dampen my courage—though I will have to admit that the latter was somewhat moist before nightfall, for the rain poured down all day long, in torrential torrents, one might say. Never before had I seen it rain so hard. I had heard of tropical rains, and this was indeed a deluge. My hat and shoes were soaked through before I had gone ten miles, but in spite of the cold, which was far greater here than in Paris, my trusty Koverall suit and woollen sweater kept the rest of me fairly dry and warm. I expected any moment that my engine would short-circuit and stop, but never once did it even skip—just kept on bucking the head wind and plowing through the mud.

ALGERIAN GYPSY CARAVAN ON THE ROAD TO TUNIS.

The first 40 miles to the east of Algiers proved to be a monotonous, flat plain covered mostly with dwarf vineyards, dotted with French villages, and traversed with caravans of heavy teams. The next 20 miles wound among scattering, black mountains, and along cactus-bordered valleys filled with wide, swollen, muddy rivers. The road on the mountain sides, always being well drained, was hard and good, but in the valleys and across the plateaux the miserable mud necessitated an unrelenting, vice-like grip on the handle bars, and an absolute concentration on the road that proved most tiring. When, added to the strong, gusty wind, soaking rain, and the rheumatic ache across my shoulders, the dangerous road cooled my motorcycling enthusiasm materially. Sign-posts being totally absent in this district, I always followed the best road running east, and to increase my misery, hard luck led me up the wrong branch of a fork, and not until I had gone 20 miles out of my way and found myself again on the coast of the Mediterranean near Dellys, did I realize my mistake.

On the Main Road Again.

The magnificent view partly repaid my dismay, however, for the angry sea whipped up by the storm broke upon the rugged headlands with such fury that the picture was full of the wildest grandeur. A tiny, dried-up old Arab who understood French happened along just then and told me the only way to the next big town on my route was by retracing my track to the fork. As he was the first member of the human family I had seen for an hour, I snapped his photo with the sand and surf for a background, as a record of my visit.

After scaring the two handsome, mustached riders of one small donkey the second time, I finally regained the main road and arrived at Tizi-Ouzou, three hours behind schedule time. Here a crowd of Arab boys followed me from the edge of the town to its center, each doing his best to pull me in a different direction to some hotel or other, and expecting a tip for carrying a bidon of "l'essance" across the sidewalk, or for "guarding" the machine from theft when I was always there.

Enters Woods Despite Warnings.

I would not wait, however, stopped only to fill up with gasoline at 60 cents for five litres (available in all large Algerian towns), to buy a big roll with a slice of ham, and a fresh box of matches, before continuing into the valley of the Seboon. After crossing the turbulent Oued Aissi, I left the Route National No. 5, and took the R. N. No. 12 to the left. From here on the country was very hilly and formed the ascent of the Grand Kabylie Mountains, which I hoped to cross lengthwise for 40 miles before dark.

Large forests of cork and oak trees bordered the steep and sinuous road, sometimes varied with gentle gradients, but always climbing and always very beautiful, revealing towering crags and deep valleys through the gusts of rain and clouds. At Azazga, where I halted to ascertain my way, the natives gave me quite a shock by urging me to go no further until the storm ceased, stating that the "neige," or snow, filled the mountain passes and made my passage impossible. But I resolved to take a look at that snow, even if I did have to return.

CHAPTER X
Clancy's Wheel Tracks in Africa

Being the Tenth Installment of His Journey
Around the World on a Motorcycle

EVEN IN THE DESERT, FAR FROM HUMAN KIND,
THE ARAB HEEDS THE CALL TO PRAYER.

U p and up and up and up the road climbed, winding around the forest-clad faces of a wilderness of giant peaks, until I began to wonder if there ever was any top, but always the road was well engineered, and warnings for the sharpest turns were posted by the Touring Club of France. At nearly every inner turn on the mountain side a foaming torrent rushed headlong down the almost vertical ravine, and then under the narrow stone bridge, to lose itself in the wold valley below. Of the latter, I could catch only occasional glimpses through rifts in the clouds, which now surrounded and darkened the road. My! How the wind did roar and sigh through those scraggly forests! Nature's grief seemed inconsolable.

At the pass of Col de Tagma the road attained an altitude of 3,093 feet, and here, sure enough, banks of drifted snow were scattered on the hillside, but only mud remained on the road. Thanking the stars that my mottos, "Never believe what you hear" and "Take nothing for granted," had prevented my tarrying at Azazga, I sped down the first descent I had met for 15 miles.

Met a Strange Cavalcade.

It was on this rapid decline, with my clutch off and my engine throttled down, that I slid suddenly around a sharp curve onto the strangest group of Arab horsemen I have ever seen. Well dressed and well mounted, what could they be doing here, ten miles from even the merest hamlet, on this wretched, viewless day? Were they highwaymen, brigands, or what? As it happened, they were as much surprised at our sudden meeting as was I, and their horses were even more so, becoming so excited that one narrowly escaped backing into me as I dodged past, while another was prevented from throwing his rider over the precipice by the merest chance. In fact, their horses kept the hands of these mysterious men so full that I was able to get away around a turn before they could take any offensive action. What my fate would have been had I been going up the hill instead of down, wouldn't be hard to imagine—with a thousand-foot cliff so conveniently by.

The descent didn't last long, and soon I was climbing again through the strange forests, past several picturesque Kabylie villages, until I had attained the great height of 3,230 feet, at the pass of Takdint. This section is called the "Suisse Africain," or Switzerland of Africa, and the panorama from here on a clear day, including the distant Mediterranean, must be indescribably wonderful. Rocky peaks towered thousands of feet above me even there, and valleys lost themselves as far beneath. Constantly I cursed my luck that the clouds and rain veiled this scene from my sight. Indeed, I felt like an aeroplanist lost in the clouds which darkened the day to almost night and often prevented my seeing over 12 feet ahead. The gloom was decidedly dangerous, too, for no fences guarded the brink of the cliffs and at the foot of a sharp descent I nearly ran into a mass of enormous boulders and smaller stones that had been loosened from their seats by the rain and slid down to the road below. As an automobile could not have passed this obstruction, one of the superiorities of the motorcycle became forcibly apparent.

TUNNEL NEAR CONSTANTINE.

A Captive in the Wilds.

From here on dozens of great bridges spanned huge cataracts which swept down seemingly from the very tip of the great mountains, singly and in pairs, to disappear in the almost bottomless valley beneath. The solemnity, darkness, and utter solitude of the scene will never be forgotten.

A road winding down the mountain side led me on through the forests of Taourist Ighil above the valley of the Soumane to the Col de Talmetz, altitude 2,335 feet, and here the night suddenly shut out the rugged sky-line and claimed me captive, 21 miles from the nearest habitation. As if glorying in their fiendish power, the rain and wind renewed their energy, but although I was chilled through and stiff as a board, I did not fear, for I felt that the road would continue good and my lamp was in prime condition.

But alas! The rain dripping from my fingers wet all my matches, except one, which the wind promptly blew out, so I had to proceed without a single guarding or cheering ray. At length it got so black that I could only creep along, and to add to my trouble a long stretch of road under repair confronted me.

With 15 miles still to go, the darkness became absolute, and brought me to a dead stop. What was I to do? I could not stay out in the storm all night on a wild mountain side 2,000 feet above the sea, aching with cold, and with nothing but a sandwich to eat since 7 o'clock in the morning. No, I must proceed, even if I had to walk.

Almost Food for African Vultures.

The next half hour came very near being my last, for, mistaking a white streak of snow ahead on my right for the roadbed, I turned for it, and not until I heard the rushing water in a gorge far down directly beneath me, did I realize that I was on the edge of a fenceless cliff. A half inch more—and the vultures would have been fighting.

Up to then my nerve had remained unshaken, but the seriousness of the situation now began to admit dismay into my heart. Still, I was too proud to walk, and crept on as slowly as I could balance the machine.

It would be hard to say how far I could have gone, had not the faint rays of the new moon rising behind the thick, black clouds, lightened the scene just enough to enable me to distinguish the roadbed from the vertical bank. A half hour afterward a light glimmered in the distance. Oh, how welcome was that spark! Then another shone out, and finally I arrived, safe and sound, in the town of El-Kseur. Never before had a village looked so good to me, and as I dried my clothes before the wood fire and drank pints of steaming coffee, I had indeed reason to be thankful. In spite of the rain, mud and darkness, I had covered 151 miles that fearsome day.

NATIONAL ROAD THROUGH THE
DESERT IN NORTHERN AFRICA.

Sixteen miles the next morning brought me to the old fortified Spanish port of Bougie, where I was much disappointed to find that I could not buy any photographs of the mountains through which I had just passed. Filling up with gasoline, I skirted the bold seacoast, through motley processions of native peasants with donkeys, bringing their produce to market (who fell all over themselves to get out of my way), for 20 dangerously muddy miles to the purely Arab town of Souk-el-Tenin. Here, as in the Arab quarter of Algiers and in the mountain villages, the town well, or spring, or hydrant, as the case might be, was one of the principal institutions of the community, the children coming from far and near with huge brass or earthenware pitchers and great bottles of goat skin for the family's daily water supply, and the women gathering to do their week's wash. Indeed, the types and customs of the people seemed very little changed from those of Bible times.

The 50 miles from here to Setif, through the far-famed Gorges of Chabet-el-Akra, and over the Petite Kabylie mountains, stand out in my memory as providing the most majestic and impressive scenery that I have ever seen. Following the right bank of the broad Oued Agrioun river over the fair National Route No. 9, ascending in easy grades, I headed straight into the heart of an imposing mountain range whose snow summits fairly glittered in the noonday sun. Up, up, up, and in and out and around the mighty hills the road twisted its way, overpowering me with superb vistas, including the beautiful narrowing river below. Lovely cascades poured down almost perpendicularly in many of the deep ravines on either side, while enormous eagles soared aloft, challenging the chattering monkeys on the rocks nearby.

FRONTIER CUSTOM HOUSE BETWEEN ALGIERS AND TUNIS.

At almost every turn I could hardly refrain from stopping to take a picture, but I waited until an indescribable panorama made further resistance impossible, and there I used my only film. Guess my disappointment later to find that in my eagerness to get a perfect picture I had over-exposed it!

Camels' First View of Motorcycle.

A little further on the road entered the celebrated Chabet-el-Akra gorges, "the most beautiful in all Africa." Imagine the gorge in the Pyrenees, described in a previous article, magnified ten times in height, depth and length, and you can form some conception of this remarkable canyon. Perpendicular rocks 3,300 feet high, backed by a multitude of others towering hundreds of feet higher, looked down upon the narrow road which for seven kilometres was cut through the solid rock itself, forcing me to dodge to the inner wall. Sometimes half the road would be washed away. Frequently I rode through heavy wooden tunnels, wisely built to shelter the road from the enormous rock slides. And always the road climbed steeply upward, with hundreds of such sharp turns that I continually blessed the day when I chose a four-cylinder motorcycle for my trip, for without my Henderson's steady, continuous power, I would have been stalled.

On one of these turns I suddenly came upon a caravan of seven or eight huge camels loaded down with semi-circular burdens of merchandise. Never having seen a motorcycle before, all these awkward beasts, as well as their drivers, became so much alarmed that I had to stop to prevent them from seeking refuge at the bottom of the cliff. These camels and a second caravan which I met 10 miles further on, were the only ones I saw in Africa, and it would be hard to guess how far they had come.

The majestic gorges continued for eight miles more, defying all human powers of description, and revealing at their extremity, which opened into a high plateau, a wonderful panorama of snow-covered peaks and forest-clad mountain sides extending for miles in every direction. So awesome was the beauty of the picture, bathed in the richest of golden and azure colors, that I passed through the village of Kerrata without even noticing it.

Deep Snow Encountered in Africa.

Here, I thought at last I had reached the top of the Petite Kabylie, but after descending a couple of winding slopes I again started a long climb, soon reaching an altitude of 2,806 feet, at Tizi-N'Bechar, and after another long descent, ascended again to the altitude of 3,608 feet, at the pass of Teniet-el-Tinn.

From this height the view back across the tremendous mountains I had just crossed thrilled me again. Deep snow, the last thing I expected to find in Africa, covered the majority of these noble giants and extended even into the deep valleys. In spite of the direct sun, the air at this altitude was sharp and cold, the most wintry I had encountered.

The natives, crowded by the roadside or standing guard over scattered flocks of half a dozen sheep or goats, seemed to feel the cold intensely—covering their heads and mouths completely, but leaving their legs and feet wholly bare. Miserable looking, repulsive faced women, often carrying children on their backs, trudged after their handsome husbands or sons straddling a donkey on ahead. But as the latter had to kick the animal with their heels constantly to keep it going, these lazy creatures might just as well have walked also.

How Algerians Travel.

The only method of regular transportation through this district is by means of huge four-horse stage coaches operated in relays and always crowded full of lordly Arabs. Were it not for their universal moustaches, these delicate-fingered idlers would have most effeminate faces. Often I would meet seven or eight of them packed like sardines into a tiny donkey cart. Others, usually older men, traveled along on foot with a kind of swinging dog-trot.

Still following National Route No. 9, past miles and miles of crushed stone dumped along the roadside for early repair, I continued through El-Ouricia down the steeply undulating slopes, past large hills of dried mud, whose surface was entirely washed away except for a scattered green bush, and through windswept valleys sparsely cultivated, ten miles more to the double square-walled town of Setif.

Another crowd of Arab boys caused me the greatest annoyance here, following me to the garage and each demanding a tip for showing me the way. One bold, half-naked youth, running alongside, grabbed hold of my handlebars and would have spilled me had I not given him a lusty kick. Needless to say, no tips were forthcoming, and the native garage proprietor had to turn the hose on the vagabonds before they could be made to go away.

Algerian Roads Like a Race Track.

After a hasty cup of coffee and the purchase of a huge roll of bread, I left Setif for Constantine, 81 miles away, at 3:30. The fact that I covered these 81 miles in three hours—the last 10 miles in the dark—is a tribute to the splendid Algerian roads—when dry. Mile after mile the road pointed ahead as straight as an arrow, and here at last I was able to turn on the full power of my engine for the first time. But only for a moment! The machine leaped and tore away so fast that I could barely hang on, and the air roared by my ears, so loud and the tears streamed out of my eyes so that I concluded 60 miles an hour was not what it was cracked up to be, and dropped back to a more comfortable gait.

My speed was so great that day and the small, sharp stones so numerous that I momentarily expected a blow-out. But my original Detroit equipment stood the strain without even a puncture, exhibiting few traces of their 3,500-mile roll over the winter roads of eight foreign countries. In fact, I had not the slightest tire trouble throughout those 650 miles across Africa.

Nearly Stranded in the Desert.

It was a remarkable speedway, that narrow road leading on and on through the desert, painted by the setting sun with the rarest blends of violet and orange, with snow-capped peaks rearing abruptly from the level plain scattered in the distance. But here I again escaped grief by the merest accident. Running carelessly over a large stone, I stopped to see what damage it had done, and discovered the hot air intake of my carburetter had dropped off, and that the connection nut on my gasoline feed pipe had jarred so loose that the precious fluid was running out in a tiny stream. Hastening to tighten it up, I again thanked the stars, for in 20 minutes more I would have been stranded high and dry in the middle of the desert!

Enough remained to carry me to Constantine, where I headed for the first hotel I saw—the Grand Hotel—being too tired after my record day's run of 165 miles to inquire prices. I never ran that chance again, though, for in the morning I had to pay $1 for my room, 90 cents for dinner and 45 cents for breakfast—or double my usual expense. It chanced to be the "swanky" hotel of the town, and that accounted for its exclusive charge.

GORGES OF RUMMEL ON ROAD TO CONSTANTINE.

Constantine, called "the city of the air," is a most unusual town of about 50,000 inhabitants. Built on top of an immense rock towering above the surrounding plateau like an island in the sea, it forms a natural fortress which is strengthened by the renowned Gorges du Rummel that deeply divide the town on the east from the neighboring hill. The city is surprisingly cosmopolitan, including large Arabian and Jewish quarters.

Rode Over "Bottomless Pit."

I would have liked to have remained here a week, but was destined to hurry on across the tremendous viaduct Sidi-Rached—the highest stone bridge in the world and nearly half a mile long—that spans the apparently bottomless Rummel gorge far beneath, to Guelma, 65 miles, and then north to Bone, another Mediterranean port, over the pass of Rasd-el-Akoa with an altitude of 2,706 feet.

Although the railroad from Algiers to Tunis passes through both Constantine and Guelma, the ancient stage-coach seems to have lost none of its popularity with the natives, and many of these vehicles remained to annoy me by refusing to turn out from the narrow road. Soon after leaving Constantine, I overtook one of these heavy wagons and, my horn proving useless, as usual, I tried to pass in the soft soil on the side. I got ahead, but upon turning back into the road the treacherous sand gave way, spilling me over just in front of the leading horses. Fortunately the up-grade enabled the driver to stop at once and I escaped undamaged, except for a smashed horn.

Further on, I passed a group of strange, round, white hills, looking exactly like huge, hollow bubbles, which, in short, they were—bubble monuments to the time when the earth's crust was nothing but a molten shell around a boiling ball.

Challenged by a Donkey.

Half an hour later, one of those numerous, horizontally-loaded donkeys, which look from a distance like a bologna sausage walking on stilts, took it into his head to race with me, starting on in front of his master at a rapid rate. Naturally, I slowed down, accepting the handicap, and followed behind for half a mile, not daring to pass. And he might have won out, had not his pack of charcoal fallen off behind, entangling his hind legs in its meshes, and forced him to sit down in a most ashamed manner. Not wishing to face the wrath of his owner, I did not stop to pick him up, but sped on beside the railway to Oued-Zenati and then via the valley of the Seybouse to Guelma.

CHAPTER XI
C. S. Clancy Forsakes Africa's Sands

**Eleventh Installment of the Story of Tour
Around the World on a Motorcycle**

From Guelma I had planned to take a secondary but more direct road to the Tunisian frontier and Beja, than the main route via Bone. The maps showed it clearly, and both at Algiers and Constantine I had been told the road was new and good. The garage manager at Guelma informed me, however, that this route had not yet been finished, and that the only way possible was via Bone, 40 miles to the north. Accordingly, I again headed for the coast, after swallowing my usual lunch of bread and coffee (milk chocolate being unavailable), and after a very beautiful ride through Heliopolis and over another lofty mountain pass, arrived in Bone in time to get my machine ready for the last 200 miles. If I could cover this distance and pass the Tunisian customs in one day, I would have my fifth day left for exploring Tunis.

Officials See First Motorcycle.

The hotel and food here were good, as they are even in small towns throughout French territories; and inexpensive, too, if one—instead of inquiring prices—states the amount he is willing to pay for accommodation, and accepts what is given him at that rate. The room will be small, but the meals will be the same as for those paying "full prices."

CRUDE HUTS IN WHICH THE NATIVES
OF SOUTHERN ALGERIA LIVE.

HIGHEST STONE BRIDGE IN THE WORLD

VIEWS OF CONSTANTINE—WHERE LES GORGES DIVIDE THE CITY

Rising at daylight, I departed from this delightful port the following morning at 7 o'clock, nearly lost part of my luggage soon after, and beat the local train to the picturesque port of La Calle, 65 miles. Here the French customs officers delayed me nearly an hour before stamping my pass. The charge was only three cents, however, so I forgave them.

A direct road led from here to Tabarka, in Tunis, but I was told I would have to cross the frontier at Ain-Babouch, so again turned out of my way. The 20 miles led over a steep, high pass, at the top of which I found several women, with their children playing about, side by side with huge, black negroes, breaking stone by the roadside. Tiny donkeys driven by the older children brought the large stones from the side of the hill in woven rope baskets hung on each side, and all day long these poor, bare-legged creatures pounded away in the hot sun.

The officials of the Tunisian Douane were most courteous, stamping my pass at once without charge, and evincing much interest in my Henderson, which was the pioneer motorcycle to pass the frontier. Automobile cross here daily, however.

While Algiers has been a French colony for eight years, Tunis has maintained its independence until recently, and still is governed by its own "regency" under French protection. On this account I did not expect to encounter such good roads in Tunis as in Algiers, and was surprised to find that, on the whole, they averaged even better. The road which led me down 12 miles to the seacoast was perfect macadam throughout.

Tunis is Safely Reached.

At Tabarka I was delayed an hour trying to get gasoline, of which the hotel proprietress would sell no less than a bidon of 16 litres. As I needed only four to take me to the next large town, I finally persuaded the owner of the only motor car in the village to let me have that amount from his tank. I also found it impossible to secure Vacuum oil, after the extra can I had brought from Algiers in my suitcase had been used up, and this increased my troubles.

I lost a third hour that day because Tunisian time is 60 minutes ahead of Algerian time, as I found when I reached Beja at five, instead of at four o'clock, as my watch indicated. Still, I resolved to keep on, and finally arrived at Tunis, 66 miles further on, at 9:30, triumphantly ending with a record of 200 miles my four-day total of 650 miles from Algiers.

The Michelin Guide recommended the "Tunis Hotel," and here I secured a large, tiled-floor room, opening onto the palm-tree court, for 50 cents, or 2½ francs in Tunisian money, which differs from the French only in coinage and design. In the morning I donned my Koveralls for the last time in Africa, rode to the beautiful central avenue of Jules Ferry—where I endeavoured to record my arrival with a photo—and then, with a small lad on in front to guide me, ran down to "the Port," where four stout natives carried the Henderson up the companionway and on board the "Solunto" for Naples, claiming 10 cents each for their reward.

Arab and Jewish Sections Unchanged.

Guy de Maupassant described Tunis as the most striking and attractive town to be found on the shores of the African continent. With over 200,000 inhabitants, consisting of 100,000 Arabs, 50,000 native Israelites, 44,000 Italians, 17,000 French and 5,000 Maltese (representing several separate civilizations) jostling each other in the streets, I certainly found it far more captivating than Algiers. Tunis seemed to me to be purely foreign. Even European influence has respected its Arab and Jewish sections, where each race and religion retain unchanged their ancient traditions and customs.

The European—or new—city, built in part of the ruins of near-by Carthage and beautifully laid out with broad avenues of fig and palm trees, provides every comfort required by numerous tourists who are attracted here by the ideal climate. But it was in the "Ville Arab" that I found the greatest charm.

Close to the Temple of Allah.

Wandering off at random, I followed narrow, winding streets under mysterious arched arcades, past dark windows of harems barred with iron gratings, and numerous tiny shops where brass utensils were being hammered into grotesque Oriental designs, and rare rugs woven on the sidewalk. Further on I was delighted to discover the Souks, or bazaars, which provide a spectacle unique in the world, outrivaling in interest the bazaars of Stamboul and the moukis of Cairo. Here, indeed, was the Orient in all its purity.

Everywhere I turned the fresh vision of an enchanted dream greeted my eyes; even the air seemed charged with the odor of sandalwood and myrrh. It was a tale of the Arabian Nights come true.

ROUTE NEAR THE MEDITERRANEAN WHICH CLANCY FOLLOWED IN AFRICA.

Soon a sign in four languages, forbidding entrance to all not professing the Musselman faith, indicated the modest doorway of the Grand Mosque, whose great inner court was screened from the eyes of "Christian Dogs" by a rude board partition. Except for this sign I would never have realized my proximity to this ancient temple of Allah, from whose lofty tower the Faithful are still called to pray to "the Prophet" each day, so closely surrounded are its exterior walls with the roofed-over streets of booths and shops of the many-colored bazaars. Here were dozens of tiny stalls not over five feet wide, where two richly costumed, dark bearded Orientals sat cross-legged facing each other, sewing industriously on fine silks, working beautiful embroidery, or executing delicate engravings on ivory, brass, and steel.

Here the open-front stores of rugs, inlaid furniture and graceful vases, which have inspired the pen and brush of innumerable artists, with their grotesque Arabic signs and curious merchants, made me wish for the treasures of Croesus, that I might buy with a free hand.

"They Thought My Costume Queer."

A long line of fig, date, and dried olive shops, tempting me with pleasures more within my means, led me up a narrow street, where I attracted more attention in my motorcycle suit than was comfortable. Several of the younger merchants called out to me, but their black, snapping eyes and dark, olive faces bore no malice, so I passed on unheeding. Women were exceedingly scarce here, and when they did appear, if of the Mohammedan faith, their faces were always hidden by two gruesome black veils, a small one extending from the crown of the head to the bridge of the nose, and a large one falling from the lower eyelashes to their waist, screening even the eyes from the contaminating gaze of foreigners. Combined with their sepulchral white vestments, these black veils made the women look shockingly ghostly.

The Arabian men, or lords of the harem, appear much more intelligent, cleanly and handsome than their Algerian cousins (probably because their many wives take better care of them) and dress quite differently. Besides their red-tasseled fez cap, shaped like an inverted bread-and-milk bowl, they exhibit a strong Turkish caste in their whole costume. And the Moorish architecture differs from the Turkish mainly in the formation of the supporting arches, and the painting of their keystone and alternating stones black. In the European town, however, French influence is almost as strong as at Algiers, the new public buildings, post office, palais de justice, and headquarters of the army being erected by the French in true designs of oriental architecture in which is not to be found any of the influence of early Spanish design or French interpretation. As the native army is trained by French soldiers, the difference between the rule of Tunis and her sister country is actually but a formality.

Patronize the Tourist Firms.

When the time came to return to modern civilization, I found I had become hopelessly lost in the intricate maze of tiny streets "burrowing" the Arab town. Not knowing a single word of Arabic, I could not ask my way, so kept on wandering until I caught a glimpse of the beautiful old palace of the Bey, or former monarch, and from there a tramcar, where I found an unveiled lady wearing the original harem trouser skirt, took me back to the Port du France and steamship office.

I had planned to go out to Carthage that afternoon, 12 miles to the north, but instead was compelled to spend it arguing with the despicable Italian officials of the steamboat line to Naples, who, having no set prices for anything—charging everyone all they can get—tried to force me to pay $20, in addition to $12 for my second-class ticket, for the freight on my motorcycle from Tunis to Naples! Contending that it was an "article of luxury," they stubbornly held to their charge, for they have no competition. But finally I succeeded in getting them down to $10, which even then was a most outrageous charge, considering that it cost me only $2 to bring the machine from Barcelona to Algiers, an equal distance and by two boats. The manager of the Universal Tourist Office (which replaces Thos. Cook & Son in Algiers and Tunis) told me later that this line was noted for its unreasonable charges, but that if I had let him handle the matter for me he could probably have been able to arrange a smaller charge. Previous experience, coupled with this one, induces me to counsel anyone who may motorcycle abroad in the future, to let the tourist firms handle all details possible. It is far cheaper in the end.

Carthage a Remnant of Ruins.

When I had given up that 50 franc note, I was in no mood to enjoy Carthage, even if it had not been too late to go there, and soon after a pouring rain commenced to tell me that mother earth sympathized with my wrath. An Englishman on board informed me later that I did not miss much for all that now remains of this great city, once boasting a million inhabitants and credited with having made Rome tremble, are scattered remnants of the ruins that have for a thousand years served as a quarry and now shelter a few miserable Arab ponies.

The grasping nature of the Italian steamboat company—the Societa Nazionale di Servizi Maritime—and especially of its manager "signori le directore" —deprived me of the expected dinner on board that night and provided an uncomfortable bunk. Following the Englishman's advice, I chose the upper berth for then, as he said, "nothing can drop in your hair." Having no competition, the "director," of course, can do as he likes, but his niggardly policy (typically Italian) is bound to be destructive in the end.

In the "Land of Emigrants."

The shores of Northern Sicily were visible through my port-hole the next morning, and by one o'clock the Solunto anchored in the lovely harbour of Palermo for a five-hour stop. Having visited here five years before, the Englishman offered to guide me about the city, so we had a fine tramp through this capital of "the land of emigrants."

The first things that caught our eyes, after we had escaped the clutches of the hotel porters and cabmen on the dock, were the queer, brightly painted donkey carts and the gay harnesses of their propellers. Whole pages of Bible history were often portrayed in gold and blue and red on a single panel, and the wheels and shafts were adorned just so elaborately. Heading at once for the beautiful cathedral on the outskirts of the city, we were rewarded for our half-hour's walk by the novel beauty of its architecture, through the interior, excepting for the original design of each of its altars, was disappointing.

Vesuvius Veiled in Clouds.

The miles and miles of lemon groves to the south of the city made this fruit so plentiful that we decided to indulge in a glass of lemonade, the first I had had for six months, upon our return to the boat through the swarthy appointed streets of this modern city.

Arriving in Naples the following morning, I found the fabulous beauty of its bay, and old Vesuvius nearby wholly veiled by clouds and rain. As the motorcycle had been included in the ship's manifest, I had to wait around on board all the morning before I could induce the mate to haul it up out of the hold. Finally the customs inspector arrived and ordered the machine to be lowered on a barge headed for the "Dogana." Feeling that I could now leave it in safety, I paid a boatman a franc to run me ashore. After having my baggage examined by the Italian customs, I took a taximeter carriage to a hotel recommended by my road guide, having nothing to comfort me but the thought that I still had a litre of gasolene in my tank.

CHAPTER XII
Around the World on a Motorcycle

The Ruins and Wrecked Roads of Italy

**Twelfth Installment of Carl Stearns Clancy's Story of
His Remarkable Globe Encircling Tour A-Wheel**

A tour of the world that did not include Italy would be like a visit to Washington with the Capitol left out. The mere mention of the name "Italy" brings at once to mind a vision of architectural wonders of great antiquity and absorbing interest, of beautiful lakes and valleys flooded with somnolent sunlight or bathed with a poetic moon; or a dream of a land of love, romance, and beauty—perhaps of the most interesting, picturesque and historical of all the countries of the globe.

Seeing Italy Without a Motorcycle.

With only a week before the departure of my boat for India, I found it would be impossible to get my Henderson both in and out of the strict Italian customs and have it crated in time for shipment, so I determined to see what I could of Italy without its aid. Upon receiving their quotations of 60 lire, or $12, for boxing and $14 for freight, and after spending a day hunting for it in the harbour, I therefore turned the machine over to the North German Lloyd assistants to be crated and loaded.

Four Cent Taxicab Fares.

Naples, the southern gateway of this land (which was, so it happened, as cold and blustering as New England on an early March day), is more noted for the beauty of its situation and surroundings than for any special interest of its own. Built on the cup-shaped base of a range of green hills bordering the harbour front, flanked by a curving peninsular on one side and rugged islands on the other, and shadowed by the appalling mass of Vesuvius frowning in the south, it is small wonder that the favourite residence of kings, emperors, dukes and princes has for ages been here.

"STAIRCASE" STREET IN NAPLES.

Monuments of their occupation are scattered throughout the city, forbidding castles and beautiful palaces, blending the mediæval with the modern; for, while old Naples I found still has its traditional narrow staired streets in the poorer sections, on the hill slopes, swarming with dirty, noisy people, new Naples, with its broad squares, smart shops and busy harbour, gives every indication of a modern metropolis.

With the aid of the cheap taximeter carriages and excellent tram-cars, it was very easy to find my way about, first of all to the National Museum, the principal tourist magnet of the city. For three cents, Tram No. 4 took me first class (which differed from second only in having thin cushions on its seats and in costing one cent more) past the enormous Royal Palace, the marble church of St. Francisco di Peolo, which combines the architecture of St. Peter's and the Pantheon of Rome, past the lofty modern arcade of the Place San Ferdinando and the imposing Castrel Nuovo, and finally through the principal business streets of the city on a belt line to the famous museum.

MODERN NAPLES WITH VESUVIUS IN THE BACKGROUND.

Besides its magnificent collection of bronzes, ceramics, and pictures of world renown, the objects of greatest interest to me here were the antique works of art, recovered from Pompeii, Herculaneum, Boscoreale, and the Roman Forum; especially the domestic relics from Pompeii—curious bronze lamps, decorative vases, jewelled brackets and heavy rings often designed in the shape of a serpent (the ancient symbol of wisdom).

Pompeii Nineteen Centuries Ago.

But most fascinating in their associations were the food products in the Salle de Comestibles. Here I found a crystalized bunch of grapes, a charred plate of English walnuts ready to serve, a half-baked loaf of bread, bowls of rice and similar grains, and many other eatables—all carbonized into immortality, and each with its own story of the end of its world.

The one thing that tourists to Naples should on no account miss, I was told, is the visit to Pompeii, only 14 miles to the south on the other side of Vesuvius; so my third day in Italy was given up to this trip.

RUINS OF THE ROMAN FORUM.

Leaving Naples by the narrow-gauge electric railway train (the conductor of which remained fast asleep, covering two seats of the crowded car with his feet until we had passed three stations), I rode out into the "campagna" through an intensely cultivated market garden district varied with climbing vineyards, past numerous stucco villages and beautiful villas of wealthy patricians overlooking the lovely bay, around the west base of sulking Vesuvius, whose barren heights (now scaled by Cook's funicular railway) were always in plain view, to Resina (built on the lava-covered ruins of Herculaneum). Then the train ran on across the lava fields of Boscotrecase caused by the eruption of 1906, to a station just outside the north "porto" of the city that disappeared nineteen centuries ago, and now reveals her streets, her houses, her forums, her baths, her theatres, her temples and her palaces just as they were laid out in the year 79 A. D., on the fatal day of her destruction.

Pompeii, founded by tribes of people called the Oscaus and Saminites, about 300 B. C., and later Latinized by joining forces with the Romans, was a prosperous provincial seaport and a favourite residence of Roman aristocracy at the time of her sudden burial, along with over 2,000 of her inhabitants.

While the lava streams of that terrible eruption imprisoned Herculaneum forever in its rocky clutches, more distant Pompeii was entombed beneath less solid strata of ashes and pumice stone that yielded more readily to the various early excavations of the ancients searching for treasure, of the French in 1860, and more extensively by the Italian government in recent days, until now one-half of the original walled city is unearthed.

COLONADE OF THE TEMPLE OF APOLLO IN POMPEII.

Exploring the Ruins of Pompeii.

After paying 60 cents admission and armed with a local guide-book, I escaped the offers of persistent guides, one of whom amused me with the generous appeal, "Please take a guide, mister; I'll only let you pay $20," and explored this famous "city of the dead" alone, almost feeling the ghost-like presence of the merry race who once thronged these narrow streets and imagining I could still hear the rumble of the gay chariots that had worn the deep ruts in the paving of lava blocks.

The streets and sections are carefully named and numbered, and for a few coppers the guardians of the best preserved houses, which are locked, admit you to their roofless interiors, usually ornamented with high reliefs on stucco walls, often brilliantly painted in vermillion and yellow, and always decorated with mosaic floors of curious design. Each house, usually of but one story, is provided with an outer and inner court (the latter containing a tiny garden equipped with a fountain surrounded with pedestaled busts of the family's ancestors) and each has its tiny alter in a niche on the wall, upon which daily offerings were made to mythical gods. In one entrance the skeletons of a father and his son in the act of flight are still preserved, and in another building (the House of Diomedes in the Street of Tombs) I saw the same long subterranean wine vaults where 28 women vainly sought refuge from the sifting ashes, as vividly described in "The Last Days of Pompeii."

PANORAMIC VIEW OF THE CITY OF POMPEII.

Making my way to the Forum, or market place of the city, I found grouped all about the beautiful temples of Jupiter and Apollo, the great Basilicas, or law courts, and market-halls for fish, grains, and all the commerce of the prosperous city. A little to the left, on the side of a hill, the great open-air theatre (seating 5,000) and smaller theatre or music-hall (capacity 1,500) are still in good preservation, and with the immense gladiatorial amphitheatre further out, attest to the pleasure-loving qualities of the populace. Numerous small cafes with their huge stone wine jars were noticed, but of especial interest was the Pompeiian "tenderloin" district, which I accidentally discovered on my ramble, as it is barely mentioned in the guide-book. The frescoes of the corner "house of the balcony" should not be missed by anyone fond of sociological comparisons of racial progress during the past nineteen centuries.

A Week Should Be Spent in Pompeii.

The public thermes and the elaborate hot and cold water baths of the larger private houses are exceptionally interesting, and when one notes the small size of the "lockers," or foot-square niches in the wall provided for the reception of the clothing of bathers, it is evident superfluous raiment was not popular in those days. The Egyptian Temple of Isis, near the small theatre, should not be missed by anyone who has read Bulwer Lytton's "Last Days of Pompeii," and a week could be spent here without fear of monotony.

It was with mingled and deep emotions that I finally returned from this city of death into life and civilization again, so hard was it to realize that nearly 2,000 years have come and gone since these same streets and homes teemed with life. Like one from a dream, I had to shake myself to awaken to twentieth century atmosphere again. "What," I asked myself, "will New York be like 2,000 years from now?"

Italian Roads Almost Unridable.

After getting several glimpses of the roads from the train, I was glad indeed that I did not make the trip by motorcycle; and here is what the Michelin Guide says about them:

"Napoli (alt. 32 ft.) to Pompeii. Leave by the barriera Ponte Madalena. Two railway bridges at 1k.

"Pazzigno (alt. 19 ft.). Branch roads, where keep straight on. Paved road out of repair, being cut up by heavy traffic, and very crowded.

"St. Giovanni a Teduccio (lat. 19 ft.). Bad paving, tramway on left.

"Portici (alt. 46 ft.). Bad paving, ruts, and holes, tramway on right.

"Torre del Greco (alt. 85 ft.). Bad paving, very slippery and muddy (caution against skidding).

"Torre Annunziata (alt. 19 ft.). Very poor macadam road. Level crossing at exit," and so on to Castelmare and Sorrento, where was laid the famous scene of "The Man from Home."

This selection is a typical description of the road situation in the whole of Italy, which is almost inaccessible to touring motorists. In fact, I learned, the roads seldom fail to live up to their bad reputation.

Cold and Dust Often Encountered.

One might classify them into two categories—roads in the plains and mountainous roads. The first are to be avoided because of their wretched condition, several of them being the old Roman roads where the huge square paving blocks (many of which have been removed for building purposes) point every which way in hopeless confusion. They are especially bad along the Mediterranean coast, where the heaps of dust encountered are very fond of clogging up one's carburetter, magneto and valve seats. When it rains, of course, this dust becomes a thick mud, which is liable to stall even a motorcycle without non-skid chains. On the other hand, the mountain roads, while very steep, are usually kept in good condition, and form the only safe highways for reaching even neighboring points on the coast.

Gasolene, or "benzina," can be found almost universally in sealed cans, but its cost is even higher than in France. As the cans rarely contain the stated quantity on account of the loss by evaporation, it is better to buy "benzina" by weight, but this the vendor will consent to only after a long argument.

The motorcyclist in Italy should protect himself against both dust and cold, as the temperature changes very rapidly, and in the mountains mufflers, ear-laps and a heavy coat are often needed, even in summer. Colored glass goggles are also desirable on account of the dazzling sun, and gloves are the only protection against mosquitoes, which will surround you the minute you stop.

On the whole, then, I was rather glad that I did not have time to make my run up to Rome, which I had planned for the last three days before sailing, via motorcycle. And it was in the second-class compartment (which, as far as I could see, differed from "first" only in the color of its upholstery and in price) of a modern electric-lighted express train that I was carried on the four-hour journey north the next day.

Rustics Live the Simple Life.

All the way the train wound among bold, craggy hills, often capped by a ruined castle which once protected the crumbling terraced town clinging to its higher slopes, and in the distance the brilliant snow-capped Appenines were always in view. And here my idea that Italy was densely populated was sharply contradicted, for only occasionally did the stucco, red-tiled towns break the journey.

The simple life of the people in the pastoral districts was indeed fascinating, but an expected impression of charm and pleasurable satisfaction at the mere fact that I was there was not realized, because my dreams had been of Italy in summer—and the Italian winter is very real.

Rome—A Hustling, Modern City.

Long before I reached the city the arches of the active and ruined aqueducts, stretching their imposing lines across the green meadows, and later the great dome of St. Peter's, towering over all, announced my proximity to the ancient capital of the world.

Rome! The Eternal City, at the whisper of whose name the earth vibrated with fear and enthusiasm for centuries; Rome, the master treasure house of art and architectural marvels for ages; Rome, without question the most historically interesting of all cities on the globe, was no disappointment.

Strangely beautiful, superbly great, Rome presented herself to me in a different one of her myriad aspects than any I had imagined. She surprised me with the disclosure that her present mood is that of a hustling modern city, the capital of the Italian government. In fact, all that now remains of Ancient Rome are, excepting the forum and Palatine Hill, scattered groups of ruins rather hard for the stranger to find. Rome of the Renaissance, I found, is the main attraction of to-day.

Breaking Into the Palatine.

However, it was to the ancient Roman forum, probably the most famous spot in the world, that I first directed my steps. From a distance, this dreary half-mile of ruins, fenced off just south of the center of the new Rome and surrounded by its buildings, requiring one lire, or 19 cents, for entrance, impressed me more like a quarry than anything else, and indeed it served as such along with the still imposing Coliseum, at its eastern end, throughout the Dark Ages. But on closer view the superb arch of Septimus Severus, the three graceful pillars of the Temple of Castor and Pollux, the huge expanse of the Julian and Constantine basilicas and the remains of the Temples of Vespasian, of Cæsar, of Vesta (or the Vestal Virgins), of Concord, and the Triumphal Arch of Titus, all rich in the history of the early ages of the civilization of man, still lay grimly awaiting my admiration. Indeed, I stood before them with awe, wondering at the greatness of the old Roman architects as lovers of the beautiful and the sublime.

New excavations are in process here, and many parties of visitors from several countries (often Americans of the noisy tourist type) were being conducted around by hurrying guides who filled them full of fabled tales. All of them, like myself, were taken in by the base graft of the guards, who, keeping the mosaic floors of various temples covered up with sand, would brush clear a square or two for a few coppers, and hastily cover them over again before the next party arrived.

As the Palatine Hill, the city of the Cæsars, immediately overlooked the Forum, I resolved to make it sight No. 2 on my itinerary, and started to climb up the same inclined plane and staircase most popular with those mighty conquerors. Arriving at the top, I was confronted without warning by a high, spiked iron fence, which forced me to the conclusion that the Palatine—like the Forum—is now a commercial proposition. Not wishing to have my climb for nothing or to have to hunt around for some brigand official to relieve me of another lire, I remembered that I was still young and hastily scaled the obstruction. Reaching the other side unobserved by the sleepy sentry, I continued through the vast sub-structures of the palace of Tiberius and Caligula, past the Casino Farnese to the park-like garden covering the top.

The Palatine was originally the Roma quadrata, or Romulean City, and from its 200-foot elevation above the Forum the buildings on the neighboring Capitoline Hill, or City of the Sabines, were clearly visible. Honeycombed with vaults and passages, and piled with ruins of palaces, temples, and basilicas where the emperors administered justice, the entire Palatine seemed but one huge monument to the glories of the past.

CHAPTER XIII
Around the World on a Motorcycle

<hr>

Clancy Slips from Rome to Ceylon
Thirteenth Installment of the Earth Tour Serial

A ttaching myself to one of Cook's parties the next morning, I luxuriated in an elegant two-horse carriage and the services of a quiet guide, upon a ride across the shallow Tiber, and past the Castle St. Angelo (Hadrian's Tomb) to visit the gem of Mediæval Rome—the Palace of the Vatican.

View from the Pope's Apartments.

The Pope's apartments command a splendid view of the entire city, the world's greatest cathedral, St. Peter's, immediately adjoins them, the Vatican itself contains in its thousand rooms more than enough masterpieces of art and sculpture for a life-time's enjoyment, the Vatican gardens are full of quiet beauty, and everybody goes to Rome to see them.

Here, also, is the world-renowned Sistine Chapel, decorated with Michael Angelo's works; a museum of precious marbles and such treasures as the Apollo Belvidere, the Grecian Discus Thrower, tapestries, the Laocoon, Mercury, and hundreds of marvels from all countries, many of whose names are familiar to every schoolboy. For the pure joy of beholding perfection and beauty, no museum I have ever seen can equal that of the Vatican.

Continuing to the southeast, past the site of the Domus Agustana, from which I enjoyed a fine view over the city—including the dome of St. Peter's—the Gate of St. Paul, the tomb of Cecilia Metella, and the nearby Domus Septimii Severi, Circus Maximus, and Baths of Caracalla, I came upon the huge stadium of Domitian sunk in the southern slope of the hill, the scene of many a valiant game and fatal contest.

Impression of the Coliseum.

The via St. Gregorio, just below, led me north under the Triumphal arch of Constantine to the familiar Coliseum, which seemed not nearly so large as it appears in photographs. The Coliseum, called the Flavian Amphitheater, was built on the site of the fish pond of Nero's Golden house, dedicated by Titus in A. D. 20 and completed by Domitian. Shaped in the form of a circle, so the spectators (numbering up to 87,000, could have an uninterrupted view of the central arena, where chariot races, gladiatorial and wild beast contests, naval battles and Olympic games were held for centuries, the Coliseum has probably been the stage of more crime and cruelty than any other single spot on earth. Its half-ruined walks and seats have been restored sufficiently to prevent further decay, and most of the floor of the arena uncovered to disclose the maze of storied caverns and passages below—the stables of wild beasts and prison of the numerous early Christian martyrs who were sacrificed here for persevering in their faith. Only when moonlight blends and shadows the ragged outline into a harmonious whole can the full impressiveness of this monument to early barbarism be appreciated. An old adage says:

"While the Coliseum stands,
Rome shall stand.
When the Coliseum falls,
Rome shall fall.
When Rome falls,
The earth will fall with it."

That night I indulged in original Italian grand opera, being both surprised at the small audience and poor acting, and delighted with the wonderful singing, which averaged far superior to that of an American opera.

A Glimpse of St. Peter's Cathedral.

Across the Tiber, St. Peter's, whose size and grandeur as a unit can be realized only from a distance, defies description. All that was great in the arts and architecture of the mediæval and Renaissance periods—all the talent and skill of Michael Angelo, Bramante and Raphael, the world's classical masters, a profusion of pictorial and sculptural treasures—all combine to make this gigantic work not only the world's grandest cathedral, but, in addition, a superb monument to the magnificence of the world's happiest era.

Built in the form of a Latin cross, but modelled very differently from the gothic cathedrals of northern Europe, and in spite of the fact that it is St. Peter's tomb, this great temple, with the worn-toed statue of its patron saint, impressed me more as a beautiful, rich place than as a house of worship. Its main portion is only occasionally used as such, not a single seat existing in its entire expanse. As a point of interest, it is undoubtedly the greatest single "object" of mediæval Rome. Yet its interior beauty, I concluded later, is excelled by that of the Cathedral of St. Paul, built upon the plan of a basilica, away beyond the Aurelian Walls, with their pyramid of Caius Cestius, on the outskirts of the city to the south.

Before leaving for Naples that evening I was privileged to see the Tiber Island, formed from the produce of Tadrian's cornfields; the one splendid remaining arch of a narrow bridge built across the same river in 200 Trevi, and the beautiful baths of Diocletian, which were at once both extensive "thermes," gymnasiums and club houses of the populace.

Knowledge of History a Necessity.

The facts that most impressed me upon leaving Rome were my extensive ignorance of Roman history, and the superficial value of my historical study at college. The only souvenirs that I carried away were a scarebus bug from the catacombs, and an intense desire to study up about all I had seen. Indeed, I cannot urge too strongly the careful study of the history of any European country by those wishing really to enjoy a planned visit.

Even a slight knowledge of Latin and Italian is also of great value to tourists, for although English is badly spoken at the hotels and restaurants—the best of which are excellent and almost as inexpensive as those of France, which they resemble—absolute ignorance of the national language is a big disadvantage here.

The Italians themselves are unattractive, yet amiable and obliging when rewarded in coin. In fact, the evil of the country is the tips. I found that as a tip is expected for the smallest amount of information, it is better to give small tips frequently; and that two or three cents is usually pocketed with pleasure. Anyone with some travelling experience need not fear the annoyance of guides or beggars—the often bemoaned drawbacks of an Italian visit.

Things That Are Cheap in Italy.

Coral jewelry and kid gloves are so cheap in Naples that I was tempted to invest heavily in presents for the folks at home, but unfortunately I was possessed at the time of barely enough wherewithal to secure my passage to Ceylon. And this remembrance also recalls the commencement of a series of most discourteous and unjust treatment that I have suffered, a description of which will, I hope, enable my brother future tourists to escape the total loss of $80 that it cost me.

Upon calling at the North German Lloyd Naples office to buy my ticket to Colombo, I learned that the custom house, or "dogana," officials had refused to permit the removal of my Henderson for boxing, and that it had lain exposed to the weather on a barge in the harbour all the week. The clerk stated that crating was not necessary for shipment, however (contrary to the statements in their literature), and that the machine would be loaded on the "Lutzow" just the same. When I came to pay for my ticket my American express check was refused acceptance by the pig-headed manager, and I was obliged to trouble the cordial American consul to identify me, after which Thos. Cook & Son cashed the check at once, although (to my regret) I was not their customer. Ultimate shortage of funds compelled me to take a chance on "third class," but even this totalled $95, which was extremely high for the mere two weeks' sail of transatlantic distance. Had I not been misled by the deceptive pamphlets, I would have taken one of the Peninsular & Orient steamers—the

English line, patronized by experienced travellers between Europe and all Indian and Oriental ports.

I had originally planned to sail from Naples to Bombay and to motor from there to Calcutta, 1,700 miles, and, if possible, to cross through China from there to Shanghai. In Naples, however, I fortunately met an Englishman who had spent the last ten years in India, and knew the road situation well. He told me that it would be absolutely impossible for a motorcycle rider to cross India, not only on account of the disconnected stretches of good roads, the many bridgeless rivers, prostrating heat and dangerous fevers, but because it would be only possible to get "petrol" in the interior at several points over 300 miles apart. (At the most I could carry but enough for 150 miles.) He stated that at the time of the "Durbar" several automobile parties had made the trip as far as Delhi, and that for them special ferries were operated and "petrol" stations maintained, but that now even an automobile especially equipped for the journey would find it almost impossible to get through. I was, however, very loath to give up the plan, and would still have attempted to follow it had I been less experienced in motorcycling over bad roads—or not been alone. As an alternative, I planned a complete tour of Ceylon and a motor trip up to Madras, in Southern India, and back, or 900 miles.

Accordingly, I headed straight for Ceylon (a crossing of Turkey and Persia being out of the question), and drew a long breath as I entered the third class division forward of the 8,500-ton "Lutzow" an hour before her midnight sailing. Fortunately, I shared a four-berth single port-holed cabin with but one other—a young English mechanic bound for Singapore—and the boat was new. Otherwise I would scarcely have survived the comfortless journey. As for the food, it was plentiful, but as lacking in quality, variety and taste as "sawdust," and a daily menu, including the butter, had to be printed in two languages by way of encouragement. Breakfast of cereal, sausage and potatoes, bread, butter and wretched coffee was served at 7:30. Dinner of soup, pork and potatoes, cold meat and dessert (twice a week of ice cream and fruit), including no butter, coffee or water, was ready at 11:30. At 3 o'clock tea, marmalade and bread were laid on the table. Supper of meat, potatoes and tea was served at 5:30, and sandwiches were available at 9 o'clock. Hot pork often appeared at both breakfast and dinner, even in the Red Sea, while fish, eggs, and salad were as scarce as ice cream. In fact, the health of the passengers seemed the last consideration, as long as they were kept full.

"JOY RIDING" IN ARABIA—DELIVERING WATER TO HOUSES

A Trip Across the Mediterranean.

The passengers were as cosmopolitan as could be imagined, including two young Dutchmen, one Dane, one Englishman, one Scotchman, one Irishman, one Malay, one German, one Scotch woman with two wee laddies, one Japanese woman, one Malay woman, and one American (last but not least). Most of them had already been on the boat three weeks, from Bremen or Southampton, and I was welcomed to complete a quartet for killing time with bridge whist. The canny Scotchman was my brilliant partner. The first night I lost a shilling bet by declaring that my cabin mate could not get out through our porthole, but I got my money's worth, because he got stuck amidships.

The first day out we passed the island volcano, Stromboli, and later Mt. Aetna, in the rear of the city, while we steamed slowly through the beautiful straits of Messina. With Vesuvius, Mt. Aetna made a total of three active volcanoes that we passed in two days. We also overtook an Italian transport crowded with soldiers for the war in Tripoli; yet so peaceful and quiet was our world the next day that it was hard to realize that thousands of men were being used to stop bullets but a little way both to the north of us, in Turkey, and to the south, in Africa. We even had ice cream for dinner.

The calm sea and increasing heat soon bore fruit in the shape of straw hats, toppees, and white canvas suits (closely resembling those of American barbers) among the passengers; and the awnings over the hatch and forecastle (our "decks") began to be much appreciated. By the time we reached Port Said, at the entrance to the Suez Canal, I was very glad to be able to invest in a huge Indian topee, or sun hat, the last thing I ever expected to own.

Four Hours at Port Said.

The English signs on the shops of this curious town gladdened my heart, as they were the first specimens of my native language I had seen for four months. And Port Said itself, the rapidly growing capital of the canal, was much more of a place than I had expected to see. It is probably the most cosmopolitan town in the world, 12 languages being commonly understood. Egyptian influence, of course, is the strongest, and Egyptian cigarettes seem to form the main export—one that is energetically pushed by native hawkers who come out to the ship in boats and quarter their prices just before the ship sails. Indian magicians operating with small chickens, fortune tellers, and post-card dealers also do a good business.

Bananas, dates, oranges and figs were, to my great surprise, very scarce here, and nowhere (including Ceylon and China) have I seen good fruit so cheap and plentiful as in New York.

A four hours' stop sufficed for a fill-up of coal and the addition of a rudder extension, and then the good ship slowly entered the 80-mile sea-level canal, built in 1865 by De Lesseps, whose huge bronze statue at its entrance, as the Scotchman said, must have cost "a bonnie penny."

Through the Suez Canal.

Wide lakes on both sides soon gave way to flat land covered with bush-like vegetation, and the desert, in all its wasteful barrenness, soon stretched away as far as the eye could see. The canal is so narrow that two large ships cannot pass unless one is tied up at the side; so with the slow speed cautiously maintained, 18 hours was required for the transit.

However, we woke up the following morning at Suez, at the head of the Red sea, where the "Lutzow" stopped for an hour to take on water and some passengers who had come down from Port Said by rail. Soon after we passed the Biblical spot where the children of Israel made their miraculous crossing of these waters.

I had often wondered why this sea is called "Red," and now determined to find out—but no one else seemed to know, either. The water itself, I can truthfully report, is as blue as the sky above it. The red sandstone cliffs that border its desert edge may give the sea its name; it might be due to the red seaweed occasionally seen in the water; or perhaps the causes are the blood-red sunsets that make the water glow like fire. But, personally, I deduced that the real reason is the fact that it is always so red-hot here, swept as the sea is by the dragon-like breath of the desert winds and boiled by the tropical sun. Anyway, we of the third class nearly perished during the three-day passage, and surely would have done so but for the air-scoopers in our port-holes and copious schooners of beer to replenish our perspiration ducts.

Sunset on the Red Sea.

The sunsets here, and later in the Indian Ocean, compensated slightly for our misfortune, with their gorgeous displays—never will I forget them. One was like a stupendous crown with alternating gold and blue points, each radiating streamers of its color clear to the zenith, where a halo of violet surmounted all and reflected the deep orange circle about the sun itself. Another was like unto a great rainbow, blending all the colors of the spectrum, which were reflected in the calm water like a rare painting in oils, shimmering on the tiny waves.

But only after the ball of the sun had slipped quickly into its watery couch, was the full splendour of nature apparent. Now like a chameleon in a capricious mood, the vivid colors would change to the softest hues. Directly over the sun the deep red would fade into orange; that would be bordered with a semi-circle of yellow, fading into one of pea-green, which, in turn, merged with a band of wonderful lavender. Next came a stretch of violet, then a ribbon of azure, followed by an expanse of deep blue through which the stars already twinkled merrily; and then outshone the new moon, chasing the few clouds away.

By the time you had noticed all this and looked back towards the sun, the sky color scheme would be again completely changed into another mixture of breathless loveliness; probably with a basis of dreamy lavender.

Aden, Gibraltar of the Red Sea.

The third evening we passed the lighthouse of Mecca and awoke the next morning at Aden, the Gibraltar of the Red Sea, a fortress that gives England just as much control over the supposedly "International" Suez Canal as if she had fortified the canal itself.

The original Gold Dust Twins (I could swear) soon rowed a welcome orange merchant out to the ship, followed closely by a number of hawkers of ostrich feathers, sharks' jaws and amber necklaces, who boarded us while we took on water and coal. The natives here are as black as night and exhibit an even larger proportion of Jewish blood than those at Suez. As it rains at Aden only once in several years, vegetation is unknown, even on the jagged mountains, and the sun reigns supreme. Even before eight o'clock in the morning I burnt my arms by leaving them carelessly exposed for only ten minutes. Of all the places I have seen Aden is the least attractive, yet here, as in most other ports, I saw a case of Vacuum Mobiloil being unloaded for the shore.

Skirting the African Coast.

For two days more we skirted the north coast of Africa, holding frequent conversations at night with passing ships by means of flashes and the Morse code, and then headed straight across the Indian Ocean.

Flying fish of all colors, varying in size from four inches to two feet in length, furnished most of the excitement during the day, with their quick, darting flights over the surface of the water to the length of 400 or 500 feet. Sometimes, I was told, they come aboard to give a sailor a black eye. At night games of "500" rivalled the music of the band in interest, and here I acquired the treasured English nickname of "the bloody Yank."

CHAPTER XIV
Clancy's Experiences in Ceylon
On His Way Around the World

Time hung heavy for my fellow-prisoners, but I plugged away industriously on my "articles," and wholly discouraged my "one towel a week" with three salt water baths each day. Every Saturday the fire drill furnished a half hour's excitement, and the day before we hit Colombo sports were arranged for the first and second class passengers. But the treatment we suffered at the hands of our stewards on the whole voyage was devoid of the slightest courtesy; and only with the greatest effort were we "English" able to obtain such necessities as washing water—things that should have been supplied without asking.

I certainly had had enough of it on board that boat by the time I reached Ceylon, yet here I was destined to run amuck with injustice in a more fatal form; but that tale must wait for the next chapter.

Landing Nearly "Broke" in Ceylon.

"Sense and seusualite hae heere stumbled on a paradise." In this quaint way Ceylon was described by Purchas in the 17th century, but its beauties were well known to the travellers of more ancient days. History records that Ceylon was poetically termed "The Flowery Kingdom" by the Chinese, the "Land of the Hyacinth and Ruby" by the Greeks, the "Pearl Drop on the Brow of India" by the Buddhists, and the "Isle of Majesty" by the Portuguese.

In recent times Ceylon has been aptly termed "a traveller's paradise," for, condensing as it does all the scenical, historical and climatical attractions of India and the tropics into one small island, Ceylon is actually a miniature tropical world in itself, capable of satisfying the mental interests of any normal man.

It is a curious experience to land in an unknown country with nothing but a "pound" in your pocket, and while I admit that I hardly enjoyed it, my sensations certainly were interesting. I hoped certain remittances would meet me here, but their arrival depended upon the receipt of my mailed requests and "certainty" was not their middle name.

Disembarking at the Colombo "jetty," I was confronted with native custom offices, who demanded to know if I had any liquor, tobacco, or firearms in my suitcase. Fortunately my Savage reposed in my hip pocket, so I was able to escape them with a simple "no."

Living in Hope of Remittance.

As quick as we dropped anchor the ship was boarded with hotel "runners" bearing cards with printed prices for accommodation. My Anglo-Indian friend, having been here before and suspecting the state of my purse, recommended the "Globe," so I surrendered my bag to its native representative (who spoke good English), and upon leaving the customs was bundled into a Rickshaw—for no European thinks of walking here—and was swiftly pulled by a black human horse to the hotel.

Resolving to live as long as I could on credit and keep my goldpiece intact, come what might, I put on a bold face and demanded the best room in the house. I got it, too (for five rupees or $1.65 a day, including meals), a cool corner room with two great windows overlooking the sea, whose soothing surf broke regularly on the beach not 600 feet away. Cocoanut palms fringed the water's edge beyond the squatting tile roofs below me, a great banyan tree reared its rounding top to my right, countless crows—the scavengers of the town—kept up a steady chorus with their hoarse cries, a queer sweetness filled the air, and when day fell with the great red ball of the sun into the ocean painted in true water colors, I had already fallen in love with the tropics.

Soon my "boy," as all the servants are called here, came in to light the gas, and my next half hour was enjoyed in watering the seven transparent lizards (varying from 2 to 7 inches in length) who inhabited one corner of the room, catching their dinner of insects attracted to the region by the light. One little fellow got a big moth-miller by the head and gulped it down in installments, wings and all. (To his credit let it be added that he quietly retired directly after.)

Meals Plentiful but Water Scarce.

Returning from dinner, served at 7:30 I nearly tripped upon a huge brown beetle closely resembling a baby elephant, and was obliged to remove my shoe to dispatch it. My bed was roofed and walled in with mosquito netting, but some clever ones that had got in first pestered me all night. I would not have been able to sleep anyway, the heat was so great, for although I did not feel unusually warm, I was bathed in perspiration continuously, and only when among the mountains of the interior did my skin dry off again.

At half-past six the next morning my "boy" woke me up with "early tea for master"—a tray of tea, bread, butter, jam and plantains; and I was busy all day trying to keep up with the other meals. Breakfast was served at 10:30, tiffin at 1:30, afternoon tea at 4:30, dinner at 7:30, and supper from 9 to 12. Except afternoon tea and supper, these were seven-course meals. "currie," or meat, rice and vegetables soaked in that peppery powder, seemed to be the featured dish—one much more appropriate for Iceland than Ceylon, I thought. Measly bananas not over four inches long, called plantains; papaya (a kind of melon that grows on trees), and mango fruits, were the only other specialties. I was kept even more busy quenching my thirst with bottled lemonade, and lime and soda, which totalled a surprising sum before I left, as water is dangerous.

Overcharged on Motorcycle Freight.

Sunday was a rather gloomy day for me, but a cablegram the following morning reversed my spirits. It was wonderful what a store of inspiration and courage came with the feeling of money in my pocket again, and the knowledge that the confidence of the powers at home continued.

The first thing I did thereafter was to try to pay the freight on my machine and get it out of the customs. Imagine my annoyance and disgust to find that the manager of the North German Lloyd Naples office had charged me over $30 instead of the quoted "less than $15" for the freight, and that the only way to get the machine out was to pay this sum. The manager of the Colombo office admitted that a mistake had been made and that the charge was outrageous, but all he would say was "We can do nothing." On top of this I was charged $3 by the wharfage company for unloading the Henderson, and I had already paid the Naples office $2.50 for loading it. Returning to the office for explanations, I was calmly told that "freight charges" never included loading or unloading costs—although the Naples office was careful not to mention this.

Friendliness of Local Riders.

Next I tackled the customs office, and was told by a Sinhalese clerk to wait in a barn-like room. Soon a lanky Englishman appeared, and the first words he said were "Are you in the habit of keeping your hat on in a gentleman's office?" Galled by his insolence I answered, "Yes, sometimes," and shut up. A painful silence followed, after which he spoke up. "Well, what do you want?" I told him that I wanted to clear a motorcycle through the customs, but that why I had been planted there and who he was I did not know. Upon this information he melted into a very agreeable gentleman—so he called himself—and, being chief of the customs, he allowed my machine to enter for the required two weeks without paying the usual 5½ per cent duty, seven-eighths of which is returned if the machine is taken out again within three months. The only government fees were "dues" of 20 cents.

After getting the machine into commission, and needing more money, I called at the American consul's office, on the top floor of a modern five-story elevator building. As the consul was out, I was cordially received by the vice-consul, who was most discouraging. He stated that the British feeling in the island against American products and especially motors was not mere prejudice, "it is actual hostility." Still, he gave me a list of prospects, and I set forth.

Motorcycles are even more numerous here than at Rome, over a dozen makes being sold in Colombo, and a large motorcycle club flourishes. Everywhere I went my machine attracted a record crowd, and several times I was stopped and asked, "Isn't this the Round-the-World Henderson?" I let several of the enthusiasts take a ride, including the president of the club, who gave me energetic assistance in nearly closing for an agency with the biggest and soundest automobile firm in the island. The manager feared my motor would overheat in the mountainous interior, and said he would sign up if it did not. Most of the machines here also have to use Brown and Barlow adjustable carburetters, so he bet me I would have carburetter trouble on my proposed trip inland. I also took the manager of the Vacuum Mobil Oil Co. for a long ride in front, in return for which he presented me with a gallon of the precious fluid.

More Trouble With Steamer Officials.

Meanwhile the North German Lloyd did me another questionable turn by refusing to allow me the through ticket rate to China. I had told their Naples office that I wanted to continue in the following boat to the Orient and followed carefully their instructions for getting the continuation rate. But, owing to a trifling technical error in these instructions, I was informed that I would be forced to pay a second local rate of $40 more than the continuation rate.

This was too much, so I ran to the American consul himself for help. I found him a most courteous and energetic individual. He told me the North German Lloyd was famous for its independence and lack of courtesy, and that my case was but one in a hundred. He knew the head man of their Colombo office personally, however, and went down with me to fight it out at headquarters.

But the stubborn German wouldn't give in. "This mistake has also been made by the Naples office, not mine," he said; "all you can do is to lay your case before our main office at Bremen in writing. After six months you may be lucky enough to have some of your money refunded." As there was no other line I could take without even greater expense, I had to buckle under again. I even tried to reserve my passage on the next boat, but was told I would have to await the receipt of her wireless after she had left Suez.

How Monopoly Abuses Tourists.

When I returned to the office two days before sailing, I found my berth had not been reserved and was told that the third class had been filled that morning. They certainly had it in for me, for upon expressing my indignation at their treatment and explaining my limited finances, the office manager had the insolence to tell me "It will be a good experience for you." The result was that I had to pay an additional $60 above the third class local rate for a second class local rate ticket. This was bad enough, but my wrath knew no bounds to find, after the "Bulow" had left the harbour, that the third-class was not full at all—not even half full.

In the mean time I managed to sandwich in a few visits about town—to the fascinating but odorous "Pettah," or native city; to the Cinnamon Gardens and lovely bungalow district; down the Colpetty Road to Mt. Lavinia, through the most beautiful and utterly foreign scenes and scenery I had yet found, and always turning out to the left in English fashion. Before leaving New York I had ordered the Goodyear Tire & Rubber Co. to ship two new tires to meet me at Colombo, and they arrived soon after I did. My old Goodyears were still in such healthy condition that I wouldn't have needed new ones for 2,000 miles more. Still, I decided to pay the $3 duty on the new arrivals and put them on, and it was with genuine regret that I parted with my old Goodyears, for they had carried me through seven European and two African countries with a total of only three punctures and one inner tube blow-out, in spite of the cold of the north and the terrific heat of the tropics.

Clothing Cheap, Tools Expensive.

This heat made me shed all the winter clothing that I had not sent home in my trunk from Algiers, and buy two white wash suits—the only clothing of the resident Europeans. They cost only $6 each, but some tools I had to buy to replace several lost or stolen cost exactly three times what they would in New York, and they were American made.

The second day I was obliged to take out a license and registration at $3 for a whole year, no short terms being provided for by law. The city hall clerks were natives, as were the many policemen who regulate the rickshaw and bullock cart traffic with the greatest care. But if you go up high enough in all public departments and in most private enterprises you will find a frosting of Europeans at the top of the cake.

Curious Habits and Costumes.

The high-caste Sinhalese (pronounced Singalese) or those of good birth always wear a queer pointed circular shell comb stuck on the top of their head of long, black, feminine hair, which, together with their skirt cloth and bare legs and feet, make it difficult to distinguish a man from a woman. Their manners are very effeminate and childish, too, but they often have attractive faces, appear far more intelligent than the Arab, but are almost as lazy. The Tamil people are most industrious and more strongly built. They make up the coolie class (although they have their own aristocracy), pull all the rickshaws, and are generally despised by the Sinhalese. Often a troupe of young Tamil girls, bedecked with earrings, nose ornaments and armlets, are to be seen carrying bricks on their heads for the construction of new buildings, carrying away the dirt of a new excavation, or sweeping the streets.

In addition, there are many Mohammedans here, distinguished by their small, round plush caps (mostly jewelry dealers); numerous Hindoos, scores of Buddhist priests, many Moors, and various classes who label themselves with round black patches placed between their eyebrows or streaks of red and white chalk. There are no American residents here, the consul told me, and the Europeans are English and German.

To "The Temple of the Tooth."

Buddhism has been the Sinhalese religion for centuries, and its career in Ceylon largely makes up the history of the island. On this account, in addition to the scenic attractions of the route, my first objective point of visit in the interior was Kandy, the last of the historical capitals of Lanka (the former Sinhalese kingdom) and the site of one of the most revered Buddhist shrines, the "Temple of the Tooth."

Leaving Colombo early one morning to get ahead of the heat, my way out of the city lay through the "Pettah," crowded with native bazaars, vegetable booths, markets, stalls, half-naked people chewing betel leaves and lime, and cosmopolitan traders from many countries. Then I swung over the great Victoria bridge, across the muddy Kelani, full of "paddy" or rice boats, and into the luxurious jungle on the other side. Here cocoanut palms, banyan, pepper, betel, and plantain trees reveled in the greatest confusion with heavy wild vines and bamboo clumps, varied with great black-limbed trees that stretched wide branches across the road, and seemed about to drop a slimy serpent upon your neck as you passed.

Tropical Heat and Vegetation.

Here in the motly shade native huts of plaited palm leaves and bamboo blended with their surroundings so well that the naked children playing in front seemed as wild as the small alligator who just managed to wriggle out of my path further on. The excellent road then led me on past village after village, requiring me to dodge bullock carts continually, through a low country chiefly given up to the cultivation of rice in shallow, square, terraced pools, now being plowed by wallowing gray buffalo; past Veyangoda, a busy cocoanut and plumbago center of 5,000 people, to Kegalia, 50 miles from Colombo. Here I purchased a gallon of gasoline for 85 cents to make up for the rapid evaporation from the furnace-like heat, as well as my normal consumption of a gallon to 60 miles.

Just beyond this important town the road climbed over a small mountain and then, running down for some distance through a most charming country, led me to the Utuwanka Pass, where a steady rise with fearfully sharp turns had to be negotiated. Now the scenery began to change. I left the rice-land behind and could easily see mountains in the distance. Still, the surrounding vegetation everywhere proclaimed that I was in the tropics, if the sweltering heat (in the sun) had allowed me to forget it.

Down a Dangerous Pass.

Soon after, I came to the foot of an apparently impassable range of mountains, over which the switch-back Kadugannawa Pass was supposed to lead me in safety. This was really the serious part of the journey, for Kandy is 1,614 feet above the sea and Colombo but 14. Practically all of the difference has to be overcome in this three miles of zig-zag rise. But I steadily pushed my way up, slowing down just enough to make the turns (which were the shortest I have ever met).

Here dense masses of forest worked their way far down into the deep ravines. On the opposite side of the valley a crashing foam-bedecked waterfall disappeared headlong into space, while above on either side the great, rugged mountains and overshadowing crags shed black blotches on the view—throwing up more vividly the wonderful light effects of the many-colored vegetation.

CHAPTER XV
Clancy's Motorcycle Rambles in Ceylon

Globe-Girdler Finds Much That Is Strange and Picturesque But Interesting

*HIGHWAY AND BYWAY SCENES OF THE TROPICAL
ISLAND COLONY—VIEWS WHICH MET CLANCY'S EYES
ON A MOTORCYCLE RIDE INTO THE INTERIOR.*

Leaving Kegalia I came to the worse turn on the island—the famous "hairpin corner," which doesn't look nearly as wicked from below as it is. But I made it O. K., and would have done so more easily had I not been so interested in the "Prophetic Rock" through which the road above is tunnelled. In the days of the ancient Kanyan kings there was a proverb in the land that so long as this rock remained intact the Kandyan Dynasty would survive; and it is a fact that not until the engineering skill of British soldiers had pierced this obstacle was Kandy conquered.

A few miles further on I came to the wonderful Peradeniya Gardens, rated as the finest botanical gardens in the world. By this time—11 o'clock—it was so hot that I decided to continue to Kandy, four miles further on, and to return here in the afternoon.

Some Flora and Some Fauna of Ceylon.

The town of Kandy lies in a cup encircled by hills. All along its front is a picturesque lake bordered with restful hotels, while luxuriant avenues of foliage surrounded its edge. Here I landed at 11:30, having covered the 75 miles in 3½ hours in comfort. I picked out a small native hotel called the "Kings," where an English circus troupe made things lively and nearly stole my American flag. I changed my clothes, had "tiffin," and about four o'clock, clad in a wash-suit, boarded my Henderson again and embarked on the retreat to Peradeniya.

Here I saw in the royal gardens, growing under natural conditions, all the tropical wealth of the Eastern world: huge Assam rubber trees with great serpentine roots, breadfruit trees, (coca) Kola trees, cacao or chocolate trees, red-cotton trees, palms of every variety, papyrus plants, giant water lilies, lotuses, thickets of enormous bamboo, and, most interesting of all, the "Bat Drive."

Four or five huge trees here are literally black with thousands of huge bats or "flying foxes," hanging by their heels—a sight unique in the world. Their bodies are as big as rabbits, and their ribbed monoplane wings seemed almost transparent as they flapped overhead in scores, filling the air with the deep hum of their countless cries. Strange to say, these queer beasts are very fond of palm wine, and frequently become intoxicated by drinking to excess from the vessels that are set to catch the flowing sap.

While I was wandering about the gardens a young English chap drove up and asked me if that was my Henderson he had seen near the entrance. I owned up and accepted his invitation to dinner at his hotel that evening. He proved to be a rubber man from the Federated Malay States convalescing from malaria here. He had heard about the Henderson from London friends, and being an enthusiastic motorcyclist, was anxious to try the machine. He was such a decent chap that I took him north with me the next morning over the terribly steep mountain road to Matale.

First, however, we visited the most sacred of Buddhist shrines, the "Dalada Maligawa," or Temple of the Tooth, enclosed by a great stone wall and surrounded with a moat. It is said to contain a tooth of the holy Buddha. This revered relic—over seven inches long—is enshrined among magnificent rubies, emeralds, catseyes and other precious stones, a striking object being an image of Buddha cut out of one large emerald. As the relic is exposed to view only on festival occasions, we had to be contented with a peek at the outside of its altar-case, and to get this our guide rudely disturbed the crowds of meek worshippers, men and women bearing trays and trays of fragrant jassamine and other sacred flowers as offerings to their god, and prostrating themselves before the altar while tom-toms drummed incessantly. Downstairs I saw one poor woman devoutly praying to a rude sketch of a rabbit drawn on the outside wall of the crudely decorated temple, which seemed in a sad state of repair.

Philanthropy Becomes Tiresome.

On many of the pillars and images of Buddha appeared patches of gold leaf, stuck there by pilgrims from Burmah in their devout endeavour to enrich the temple. In the library, long, narrow books of hand-inscribed palmleaf strips bound with wood inlaid with precious stones vied with each other in antiquity. An eight-inch image of Buddha carved out of a single crystal was also shown us, but for every little service as well as for our guide we had to pay handsomely.

At the gate a crowd of prosperous beggars loudly clamoured for additional handouts, but our generosity had been exhausted, so we climbed upon the Henderson and sped out three miles to Katagustota to see the tame elephants quartered there. These huge brutes, papa and mama about 80 years old and baby about 15, are all that now remain of a huge troupe of war elephants maintained by the ancient Kandyan kings, and are used only in religious festivals. Scores of wild elephants are annually caught in the jungle and tamed, but they are all shipped to India for heavy work.

Quietly eating their morning hay among the trees by the river, these intelligent beasts seemed very much at home and appropriate to the scenery. Small children soon crowded around to sell us green bananas, which the elephants thrust into their mouths skin and all without ceremony. Then, directed by their keepers, the mammals bowed, kneeled, stood on two legs, and did several other stunts that would qualify them for a circus. But the greatest treat was still in store for us—a bareback ride on "father." His keeper suggested it, and we took him up. First the keeper climbed on his roof and swept off the bristly back with a stiff broom, then he beckoned us to ascend.

Motorcycle Riding Preferred.

The kindly brute, the largest I have ever seen, suspected our intentions of boarding him, so held out a front leg for me to mount. Then he raised it up until I could grasp the tip of his ear, up the edge of which I climbed hand over hand, past his small, merry eye, until I could reach the chain around his neck and scramble up upon his broad, flat back. A like courtesy was awarded the Englishman, who was soon up behind me, and then, with the driver atop the huge head in front, the ponderous mass began to move! Everything had been O. K. up till then—the mountainous body feeling as solid as a rock; but now the thick skin began to slide to and fro and back and forth in a most alarming fashion. Indeed, it seemed that I was trying to straddle a young earthquake. The miniature mountain-ridge that formed the heaving backbone had it in for the Englander, but before long we became more comfortably adjusted. Our speed was not so great that we could not enjoy the landscape as it wandered by, but then our momentum was promising and our steed smelt of great reserve power.

I could almost fancy the tiny eye winked a smile at me as I clambered down upon the raised foot again, but whether a smile of indulgence or disdain I could not tell. Yet I am sure this great animal felt very magnanimous in condescending to amuse such insignificant creatures as we.

Returning to Kandy for petrol (80 cents a gallon), my passenger looked in vain for the long hill we had descended on the way out. The Henderson had taken it so easily, in spite of its doubled load, that he had not recognized it, and the Englishman was dumbfounded. As he desired to accompany me to the terminus of the railroad line, we parted from Kandy again at 10:20 to follow a narrow jungle road through dense tropical forests, past numerous cocoanut groves, rubber estates, tea fields, paddy ponds, scores of native settlements, and hundreds of bullock sarts, then over a murderous mountain pass, where the heat would have melted any ordinary engine into pudding, and finally to Matale, where we stopped at the Rest House for breakfast at 11:30.

Where Everything Is Charged For.

The government rest house is an admirable institution that has been established for the accommodation of the traveller in nearly every town throughout both Indian and Ceylon, where no good hotel exists. Most of them provide both food and shelter, but a few of the more isolated ones afford shelter only. The one at Matale was typical, making none of the pretentions of a hotel, yet a veritable house of rest. Back from the road among shady tamarind trees, a spreading one-story bungalow fronted with a wide veranda and flanked by red bedroom wings, was approached by a well-kept semi-circular driveway. The dining and living room, ceilinged by the stained timbers of the roof itself, occupied with the tiny kitchen the main building, while at the rear the automobile stable was reached by a path through the courtyard garden.

While the cook was preparing breakfast, "No. 1 Boy," or the native in charge, brought us huge glasses of lime-juice and soda (but, as usual, ice was lacking), also the government rate card for inspection. First of all came the charge for occupation—one-quarter of a rupee, or 8 cents, for a half hour; one rupee, or 33 cents, for a day. This covers a wash-up, privileges of the house, etc., and is always made in addition to whatever other charges there are. Then comes bed, bedding (it is customary to bring your own), lights, baths, early tea, breakfast, tiffin, afternoon tea, dinner, drinks, extras, garage, and servants (for many people bring their personal servants with them). Every little thing is charged for separately, and while a good meal is usually provided for 50 cents and a room for the same, I found that rest houses in general (whose charges vary in different localities) did not deserve their reputation for economy. Still, they were much more clean and satisfactory than the native hotels, and are supposed to charge cost prices.

How Have the Mighty Fallen.

During our meal a small boy pulled a huge swinging fan to and fro above our heads, a charge for the breeze from which was, of course, included in our bill.

Just as we had finished, an American globe-trotter whom I had met at Colombo blew in with a native in European dress at his heels. At once my companion cleared out, while my countryman sat down to write his university for some agricultural catalogs for the native. After our salutations had passed, I followed the Englishman to learn the cause of his sudden exit. "Isn't your friend a bit weird?" he asked, "to hang around with natives like that, and especially to bring them onto a room with gentlemen?" And this one sentence illustrated beautifully not only his attitude, but the attitude of all the English people toward the natives in all the English colonies I have visited. Their idea is that education spoils a native—that he must be "kept in his place" or else he will become insufferable. They resent his "imitation" when adopting European clothes, and discourage most of his efforts to better himself. In all of Ceylon I came across but one school, and was not a little disgusted at the way the heavy-drinking English "planters" aristocracy conducted themselves—ordering around as if they were dirt under their feet the descendants of a race who had ruled royally before England had been discovered. The Ceylonese as a whole are in about the same condition as they were when England took control of the island.

CHAPTER XVI
Clancy's Night in A Ceylon Jungle

**American Globe-Girdler Unwittingly Arouses
Chorus of Wild Beasts But Finds Much That
Is More Interesting if Less Exciting**

Learning that the gasoline supply in eastern Ceylon (originating in Sumatra) is most unreliable, I sent a paid reply telegram to the rest house at Dambulla, 29 miles ahead, to learn if they had two gallons in stock and to reserve it. The reply was three hours in coming, but it was satisfactory, so I lost no time in parting with the young Englander and covered the 29 miles in 70 minutes. Upon arrival at Dambulla I found it was very fortunate that I had telegraphed, for an automobile had called but half an hour ago and endeavored to buy all of their scanty seven-gallon stock—the only petrol in thirty miles.

Why Dambulla Caves Are Temples.

Forming an impressive background for the double row of mud huts that compose the village is a solitary mass of black kneiss that rose from the plain to a height of about 500 feet. Curious to see the famous rock temples located near the top, I engaged the rest house guide for one and a half instead of his requested two rupees and started on the ascent. At the top of a steep, well-worn stairway cut in solid rock, and back of a wide, deserted ledge ending in a deep precipice, a series of caverns formed by walling up the mouths of great caves came suddenly into view. After hallooing down into the valley for the priest to send up the keys to the temple, the guide told me that in their natural state these caverns were selected as hiding places by the Sinhalese King Walagambahu (I had to write it down) after he had been driven from his throne at Anuradhapura by the Tamils in the first century B. C. After 15 years of exile he managed to regain his throne, and in gratitude for their protection, transformed the caves into temples, which they have been ever since.

RUINS IN ANURADHAPURA.

Mid Statues of Buddha and Frescoes.

A handsome, curly-headed boy, followed later by the priest himself and two monks, then arrived from the depths with the keys to the largest cave, and soon I was fascinated by the weird and grotesque scene inside. As my eyes got accustomed to the dim, mysterious candlelight, I discovered that the temple was inhabited by scores of Buddha's images—varying in attitude and size from a recumbent statue 46 feet long, carved out of solid rick, to a seated wooden figure four feet in height. Ranged around the oval circumference and grouped in circles in the center there were 54 of them in this cave alone (156 in the whole five). All were highly decorated with gold and enamel paint, and all said never a word. It was highly disconcerting to be staring at one and suddenly find you had been leaning against the nose of another.

ON THE ROAD TO METALE.

The frescoes that literally covered the low rock roof in many colors were also of absorbing interest—including, as they did, a strange mixture of Brahmin and Buddhist images and pictures of historical scenes (one occurring in 543 B. C), and with a sprinkling of Hindoo influence for seasoning. Many of the frescoes were over 2,000 years old.

SIGIRI ROCK, DAMBULLA.

Mysterious Spring of Sacred Water.

But the most curious thing of all was the sacred spring of water which dripped slowly in crystalline pureness from the roof of the cave into a jar below. No one has ever found from whence this water comes, how long it has been dropping, or why its mathematically regular fall never varies throughout the year (in the long, hot summer or during the rainy winter season). Because of this mystery the water is sacred and no human must drink it.

The plentiful supply of Cyclopean objects of worship were not a bit congenial, so I was finally very glad to pay the corrupt, sneering priest my disappointingly small "offering" and escape from the eerie feeling of that strange dimness into the sunshine outside. I had still to rub my eyes to get rid of the uncanny vision of that fearful cave.

PALACE RUINS AT ANURADHAPURA.

The landscape that burst into view from the ledge aided these efforts. Ranges of ragged lined, tea covered mountains stretched away over the Kandyan mountains in the gray distance to the south, beneath lay the rice fields granted by the ancient kings for the temple's endowment, while in the center of the jungle to the east the great rock of Sigiri rose in solitary grandeur to beckon me on to the night's resting place at her foot.

ROYAL BATHING PLACE OF PRINCE KASYAPA,
BUILT ABOUT 450 A.D.

Returning, I first met a fair young priestess and further down, a boy priest bearing keys to the minor caves. They had seen my shoeprints in the sand and were making the arduous climb with the hope of a few pennies reward for their pains. Reaching my patient Henderson again at 6:30, I found I would have to go some to make the additional 11 miles to the rest house at Sigiri before dark.

In the tropics the sun is so nearly opposite the equator and the angle of refraction so slight that there is, strictly speaking, no twilight—darkness falls upon the heels of the sun. I had noted this phenomenon night after night since leaving Suez, and now the interval between sunshine and blackness lasted scarce 15 minutes.

A Dangerous Ride in the Jungle

Learning of my intention to reach Sigiri that night, my guide and the rest house keeper loudly clamoured against this "folly," stating that the wild animals came out into the road after sundown and that it would be exceedingly dangerous to enter the jungle before morning. They even added that I could not hire a dozen coolies to make the trip in a body—while I was alone.

"What is the danger?" I asked. "Rogue elephants (those that have been wounded by man), cheetahs (panthers), bears, wild buffalo, etc., etc.," they replied. "All big game," I thought to myself. "Well, I'll chance it; I hate to give up what I've started out to do."

Digging my "Savage automatic" out of my hip pocket I primed it carefully and slipped it into the right outside pocket of my koveralls. Then, after seeing that my lamp was O. K. (I had purchased a new one at Colombo—my fifth), I started off amid a chorus of protests, shouting "Sigiri or bust!"

For the first five miles the jungle road was good, the light fair, and the only animal to show up was a jackal. Then my way branched sharply to the right—evidently a new road, little used, narrow, winding, grass grown and deep in sand; not a track conducive to speeding even in daylight. But I dashed on, and then the darkness fell suddenly. I did not want to stop to light my lamp, fearing that the light might attract the fool animals, nor did I want to spend the time.

But what was that bulky mass in the road ahead? A rogue elephant surely, I thought, "the only kind that will attack a man." What should I do? I couldn't turn around now, and I might be almost there. No, I will rush him and try to scare him first; let him charge me if he will. All these thoughts flashed through my mind in an instant, and then—Oh, how I wished for a muffler cutout, the first time I had ever wanted one! I would have swapped my birthright for it. I didn't even know whether wild animals were accustomed to turning out to the left or to the right.

Where a Puncture Meant Destruction.

Blowing my horn like mad and opening wide my throttle, I charged the monster with wild yells, and succeeded, as I had hoped, in sending him off snorting and crashing into the thicket. Coming abreast of him I was a little disappointed but not much relieved to find that he was a wild buffalo—not an elephant—for the former is almost as wicked. A longer five miles I've never known and never hope to see, than that black, sandy path winding and winding through the jungle. "What would happen," I thought, "if I had a puncture?" Only one more buffalo blocked my road that night (this time I was sure it was an elephant), but I must confess that my nerves were anything but calm when I suddenly brought up at Sigiri, startling the two lady guests with my unhallowed arrival. Nor did I need to be firmly admonished that I "ought to be thankful that I had got through alive."

A wash-up, change of clothes, and a good dinner with Australian butter served in tin cans, sufficed to recall my dignity, and then I went out to see the Sigiri Rock loom up like a black giant before the rising moon, challenging me to climb, and to sense the atmosphere of the place—to try to feel that I was really there. Situated in the center of a little square clearing, edged with a barbed wire fence, the Rest House formed a veritable "corral" in the jungle—an oasis in the wilderness that was once the heart of a wonderful city. Unlike the others, its main room was only half walled, like the divided door of an Irish farm house, so the cool breezes and the mosquitoes, magnetized by the chimney candle lamps, had full sway.

A Night With the Jungle Chorus.

Discovering a history of the place, I read until these swarming pests nearly devoured me, and then retreated to my ground floor room. Placing the candle on the bureau, I continued to read until midnight, when I suddenly extinguished it and retired in the dark. Foolishly I had not noticed the low open window beyond the dresser, and for two hours the candle's steady beam had been shining straight into the jungle. The result was an audible gathering of all the wild beasts in the district—much to the terror of the growling watchdog and to my later uneasiness. Separated as I was from the jungle by a mere wire fence, a flimsy window curtain, and the mosquito netting around my bed, I momentarily expected two luminous eyes and a dull thud would announce the arrival of some inquisitive four-footed visitor, and I clenched the cocked ten-shooter under my pillow. The chorus of weird sounds outside made the very thought of sleep impossible. Panthers snarled, bears roared, elephants trumpeted, jackals bayed, owls screeched, bats flapped, and buffaloes snorted—until there was no peace within me.

Finally the long night wore away and daylight abruptly came to my rescue, rousing my guide for the scheduled early morning climb of the remarkable Sigiri Rock. He wanted two rupees, or 66 cents, for the job (the fixed government charge), but I had been told that a guide was not absolutely necessary, so informed him that one rupee was my limit, and if he wanted to go for that he could. Arguing that there were over 750 steps to be climbed, he refused, so I started off rapidly alone. As I had figured, one rupee looked better than none to him, and he caught up to me within half a mile.

Historic Home of a Patricide.

Soon passing the coolie huts of the Archaeological Commission of the Ceylon government (now exploring and restoring the ruins) arranged in a quadrangle for protection against prowling wild beasts, we advanced upon one of the most romantic and fascinating spots in the Old World, making a striking picture as the warm, red tones of the cliffs beamed a welcome in the early sun. This was echoed by the lighter hues of their reflection in the ancient artificial lake at the crag's foot, where we looked for crocodiles that bask in the sun, and saw where elephants come to drink.

About the year 475 A. D., a fiendish Sinhalese prince named Kasyapa, who had killed his father to obtain the throne, and rendered himself unpopular by other crimes, dared no longer to live openly at Anuradhapura, the ancient capital, for fear of his brother's revenge; so he retired to the rock of Sigiri and strongly fortified it. (One of the ruined outer ramparts included the rest house.) The perpendicular sides of the rock—over 400 feet high—made climbing impossible, but the clever Kasyapa constructed a balconied stairway gradually winding around it from base to summit. Upon the four acres of the top he built a splendid palace and administration building, and lived in great luxury until his Buddhist conscience began to trouble him. Later, his brother's overwhelming army cut his own to pieces and frightened him into suicide. Thereupon his brother wrecked the fortress and returned to the North.

Several long flights of stone steps remained to lead up the terraced slopes to the foot of the cliffs, where the rock foundations of temples and houses, and huge bath tanks cut into the tops of great boulders, were clearly to be seen. From here we mounted restored stairways of stone and iron to the foot of the original inclined walk, part of which yet remains. Now a wonderful view opened out of the lake-like mist settled over the jungle for miles around, with the mountains protruding like islands in the distance.

Longing for Sight of a Pretty Girl.

Forty-five feet above the center of the stairway was a pocket or shallow cave in the rock which the guide said contained some excellent frescoes of Kasyapa's ladies, to be seen if I dared to risk the shaky climb up the wire and bamboo ladder that hung perilously on stays driven into the face of the rock. "Are they pretty?" I inquired. (I hadn't seen a pretty girl for two months!) "Master go see," he grinned. So, as usual, I took a chance and tested my nerves to the limit as I slowly crawled up the ladder, swinging clear out beyond the jutting rock over a sheer 300-foot drop. Finally the ancient guard room, or "look out," was reached, and I was glad I came. Here were fresecoes of several ladies 430 years old (I mean the frescoes), with colors and lines bright and fresh in spite of their exposure to the monsoons of 15 centuries—real exposure, too, for they were bare from their waists up, except for sundry necklaces and smiles. And those waists! —a 14½ collar would fit beautifully. Speaking of complexion, you wouldn't take them for over 19, were it not for their grotesque hair-dress and queer expressions (slightly embarassed). They were no beautiful "queens," yet their skin was remarkably light for the climate. Still, I would recommend that climb up that ledge to any bachelor adventurer, with emphasis upon the giddy descent which was a 45-foot thriller. You feel like a young steeple-jack!

A nine-foot wall that was built on the outside edge of that ascending gallery to protect its users, had an inner surface as polished and almost as hard as marble, yet it was only catted with "chunan," a kind of cement so well preserved that I deduced there was little graft in those days.

Sigiri Soon Will Be Famous.

This overhanging balcony led on and up around to the terraced north side of the rock, where half the foundations of ancient buildings remained on the rock, the absent half having been supported by mere temporary sub-structure. Then a long, new iron stairway mounted to a wide ledge—once the site of a temple—where the Archaeological coolies would soon be at work. Now the ancient grand staircase, partly restored, led up its terraced flights between two colossal lion's paws and fore legs, masoned of huge bricks and mortar. At the lion's chest the original steps ended and zig-zagging iron stairs led directly to a second ledge. From here the footholds were the original foundation drillings for the great buildings of the top, the danger of slipping being guarded by an iron hand-rail.

Breathless, I arrived first at the top, only to find four acres of what seemed at first glance the half-sister to a brickyard. Further exploration revealed four great bath tanks cut out of the solid rock, still full of rain water; a large couch—the king's—carved out of the rock; a flight of stairs in quartz, courtyards, passages, and many other evidences of royal diminion.

The view was magnificent—in itself enough to attract the crowds of people from all over the world who are expected to visit here as soon as the story of Sigiri becomes generally known. After the descent, which took only half an hour, I hurried back through the jungle and on to Habarana, to make the most of the cooler morning hours.

Through the Jungle to Polunarawa.

The ruined, or buried, cities of Ceylon, which are much better preserved and known to science than the similar ruins in India—

if not older—were the attractions that brought me into this torrid wilderness. The principal of these is Anuradhapura, the Sinhalese capital from about 1000 B. C. to 500 A. D., and Polunarawa, the mediæval capital, which bloomed in the twelfth century. Tracing history backward as I was, it was seemly that golden Polunarawa lie next on my route, or but 27 miles off from it. At Habarana, therefore, I turned east through the unbroken jungle for the hour's run over a good but little used road.

All the tropical vegetation of the south had now disappeared. The palms, rice, rubber, etc., and much of the roadside reminded me of a neglected New England forest. But the jungle was alive with wild animals and evidence of their proximity constantly was at hand.

CHAPTER XVII
Ceylon to Hong Kong With Clancy

World Tourist Gathers Considerable Data
Concerning Riding Conditions in "New" Fields
And Corrects a Few Warped Impressions

BRIDGE AND TEMPLE NEAR PEKIN.

TYPICAL ROADS IN CHINA...

...AND THE WAY TO TRAVERSE THEM.

At the 14th mile I reached the lovely lake of Minneria, one of Killarney's rivals, whose islands have not been explored for a thousand years. Myriads of curious birds—some of great size—darted away with the spotted deer at my approach, but the lazy crocodiles continued to bask in the sun on the beach.

Long before I reached the rest house of Polunarawa, on the banks of another charming lake (originally artificial), several of the noble remains of its old and splendid civilization appeared by the roadside. Most of the ruins of both cities are religious monuments.

Polunarawa in Days Gone By.

Polunarawa was blessed during its happier days with an able ruler, "Parakrama the Great," the greatest of Sinhalese kings. This beloved man would honor his victorious battles or abundant harvests (largely the result of his extensive irrigation systems fed from huge artificial tanks or lakes) by submitting to a second or third coronation, after which he was accustomed to celebrate by building some huge dagaba or a temple to his prophet Buddha, or a giant image of him who had prospered the land. One of these monuments is the Polunarawan Dalada Maligawa, or Temple of the Tooth—Buddha's tooth. (I am not sure whether it was his only one, but it is the same baby elephant's tusk that has been chased around all the old cities from Burmah to Kandy—where it now reposes—from time immemorial.

Ruins Inhabited by Apes.

Another temple is the massive Thuparama, built for the relic called Buddha's collarbone—also a traveller now at Anuradhapura. A third is the Jetawanarama, an imposing pile 170 feet in length with 12-foot walls 80 feet high, and supposed to be the temple of Buddha himself. Built of red brick, it was originally plastered with chunan, which still makes light patches upon the warm tones of the crumbling brick. A dilapidated statue of Buddha 60 feet high faced the entrance of two polygonal columns, and the whole has a most crestfallen appearance.

I found a little stucco Buddha leaning against the wall of his tiny niche so forlornly that I brought him along with me for company. Homesickness has now broken him all up, but I still cherish the remains.

The distinct feature of the Polunarawan buildings is the Hindoo character of their exterior, which curiosity is unexplained. Having seen all that was to be seen, I decided to hurry along and make my next stop at Anuradhaupra, the original and best known of these rich cities, which abounded, as did Polunarawa, in theatres, bathing halls, gardens, fountains, public buildings that shone with roofs, doors and windows of gold, and palaces whose splendour has never been excelled. A short description of the architecture of the ancient city will give you a good idea of the latter as well.

While wandering about these jungle-embowered ruins, I came upon a troop of huge gray monkeys—almost man size—with black faces and long, black tails. They leaped to and fro among the trees and stopped to make faces at me. I pulled out my Savage, intending to scare them with the noise of its report, but my guide protested. He said that if by any accident I should hit one of them that the whole troop, about a dozen, would rush for us and tear us into bits. If they are not molested, however, these fruit eating apes are harmless.

Viewing Penang from a Rickshaw.

I spent the night at the excellent rest-house here, having the same company that I had the night before at Sigiri—an old planter's wife who was touring with her maid by automobile, and who regaled me with stories of the good old days in Ceylon, "when there weren't no Ten Commandments, and the best was like the worst," as Kipling put it. In the early cool of the following morning I returned to Habarana—stopping en route to try a shot at some snipe and jungle-fowl—and then continued through 38 miles more of lonely forest to Mihintale, very nearly taking a wheel off a tawny panther which crossed my path and dashed into the thicket so hurriedly that I judged he had a guilty conscience. Often the natives would reverently salute me as I passed, believing me some kind of a god or demon.

IN THE FEDERATED MALAY STATES.

Ceylon is a good place to buy gems cheaply if you are expert enough to be able to tell a "white sapphire" from cut glass—otherwise you are very apt to pay several dollars for one of the five-cent stones that are shipped here from France by the barrelful. But the best place of all to buy is on shipboard during the last half-hour before your boat leaves Colombo. Then the native jewelry dealers who swarm the ship will sell really good stones—if you can pick them out—at ridiculous prices. The Anglo-Indian who came on board to see me off knew moonstones when he saw them, and together we bought a lovely necklace with 56 stones, a five-stone pennant, an eight-stone pin, and a five-stone sapphire ring for a total of $13.25—jewels that would bring ten times that sum in New York.

On the "Bulow" I was in Deutschland again, but a girl from Illinois and two young Scotchmen appeared to liven the bunch, so the pain of further North German Lloyd associations was lessened. Like a Scotch lass bound for Singapore, a German maid going to Shanghai, and an English girl for Hong Kong, this American girl was going out to be married. It seems that all the Australian boats and most of the Oriental liners usually carry a fair cargo of prospective brides, travelling alone. The voyage was a long one, however—those five weeks from Southampton to Shanghai—and from several impromptu romances I observed during the latter two weeks of it—well, I should not want a wife of mine to "come out" that way. There were also a young English woman and a French girl, both with children, returning to their Chinese husbands in Hong Kong, and two more miserable souls I never hope to meet. Later I heard both their "stories" —powerful descriptions of the way Orientals regard their wives; tragic tales that made the horror of international marriages unforgettably apparent.

PRIMITIVE ROAD BUILDING METHODS
ARE EMPLOYED IN SINGAPORE.

I found second class much better than third in food, but not enough better in either service or accommodation to warrant the additional cost. A four-days sail across the quiet Bengal Bay, "on the road to Mandalay, where the flying fishes play" (great big blue ones), brought us around the north end of Sumatra to Penang, the northern metropolis of the Federated Malay States, an English colony since 1874. I hoped to be able to get off here and motor down the peninsular to Singapore, and catch the boat again there. Careful inquiry informed me, however, that this would be impossible, for the roads, which were perfect as far as they go, extend only as far south as Malacca, or 150 miles short of Singapore. The remaining distance—a swampy jungle—could have been covered by boat or train, but poor connections and the limited time precluded even this arrangement.

The information I gathered from motorists both here and at Singapore will be of value to anyone planning a trip through this interesting country, and blessed with plenty of time.

In the Federated Malay States the newest West is found side by side with the ancient East. The mixed population is largely Chinese, and all the rickshaw coolies were yellow men. The typical Malay seems to be a mixture of Chinese and monkey, and is about the most unreliable person on earth. Arriving in Penang (Georgetown is the name of the city and Penang is the island) in the early morning, one of the Scotchmen and I took a rickshaw—which seat two here—for an exploration of the city. As we wheeled along the squalid streets of the business section we passed dozens of stuffed pigs, roasted turkeys and trays of all kinds of sweetmeats being borne on the shoulders of pairs of trotting Chinamen. Our curiosity aroused, we inquired what feast was in progress and learned that this procession was only part of the preparations for a Chinese funeral. A rich old lady had died, and this food was to be buried with her for the nourishment of her spirit, poor soul!

Further on we passed several young Chinese girls being drawn to school in rickshaws, and then came to the residential section. Here, surrounded with velvety lawns shaded with flowering trees, amid a somnolent air perfumed by great clumps of varied flowers, bungalow after bungalow was stowed away, vying each other in comfort. The level, hard road was bordered by red-blossomed ironwood trees and palms, and the sea lapping the shore beyond made the whole place seem running over with beauty and ease. Soon several motorcycles raced in, bringing their riders to business, and them I followed for aid and information in executing mine.

"Yes, there are over 2,000 miles of fine roads on the west coast of the peninsular," they said, "but you can't motor to Singapore; there is no road beyond Malacca." One cultured chap, a rubber man, was especially courteous. Among other facts, he told me that there is no import duty on tourists' machines entering here—only a wharfage fee; that residential licenses were pretty stiff, but not the tourist's; that there is no speed limit except that required by the roads—which are somewhat narrow, and traversed in many places by an unending procession of bullock carts and numberless sharp corners; that there is little difficulty in obtaining petrol (Shell Motor Spirit, a Standard Oil product made in Sumatra, costing 40 cents a gallon here); that 70 to 90 degrees in the shade is their average temperature, steady all the year around; that from April to September is the best time for a visit on account of the heavy rains of other months; that more than a six-inch clearance, a canvas night covering, and a large cooling system were necessary for automobiles; that a slight knowledge of "Malay" is essential, because of the numerous similar-looking roads and great scarcity of signposts; that I would need a special pith sun helmet and dark glasses; that the hill roads were dangerous and I would have to watch my brake, but that the magnificent forest and jungle scenery, and splendid cultivation of rubber, rice, and cocoanuts would make the trip to Malacca very worth while. Half the world's supply of tin comes from here, also, he said, and that a visit to the mines is very interesting. All of which made me very sorry to be prevented from going through the Federated Malay States.

Cricket and Football Played Daily.

A sudden downpour of rain caught us before we returned to the boat, proving that it can rain here in April also. Soon after its end we were sailing gaily down the Straits of Malacca on the day-and-a-half run to Singapore. Although this pass between Malacca and the Federated Malay States looks like a river on the map, we were out of sight of land for most of the way.

Singapore is the metropolis of the South Sea Isles—the commercial distributing center for Sumatra, Java, Borneo, and Australia. Its splendid harbour is approached through a nest of small islands through which a special pilot was needed to steer us. As the passenger wharf is three miles from the city, the members of my landing party took a "garry," or small coach, and drove up to town.

The chief characteristic of Singapore seems to be that it is rapidly growing, for everywhere the ground and streets are torn up for new piers, new hotels, new gas pipes, etc. The native town held no special interest—except its "Malay street," which presents each evening a sight unique in the world. The European town—English, as usual—boasted some fine hotels and business blocks; but the most attractive spots in the city were the wide recreation grounds where cricket and English "football" is played daily.

Near the Equator, Yet Cool.

We indulged in dinner in one of the bigger hotels, tasting nearly all of the 24 numbered dishes, and could hardly believe, as we strolled about town in the cool of the evening, that Singapore is less than 100 miles north of the equator. Strange to say, however, the heat is never so extreme here as in cities much farther north, holding a steady average of 80 degrees the year around. As in Penang, there were many motorcycles here, all English makes.

Before the boat sailed the following noon, I managed to dig up the following information about roads in the near-by islands of Sumatra, Java, and Borneo, which, with Celebes and New Guinea, form the profitable Dutch East Indies. Sumatra covers just twice as much territory as the British Isles. Padang, on the west central coast, its principal city, is reached by small steamers from Singapore, Penang, and Batavia. The island is covered with good Dutch roads, and petrol is plentiful and cheap. Numerous volcanos and rare tropical scenery form the principal attractions, but the capitalist is more interested in the ideal conditions the climate of the mountainous west coast offers for rubber culture.

Java, "one magnificent garden of luxuries," is much better known to the tourist, and everyone who has visited there seems enthusiastic over its charms. One man put it, "Java fulfills my preconception of what a paradise ought to be." Java is a little larger than Cuba, and is so mountainous that, in spite of its proximity to the equator, its climate is like ours in spring. Eight of the mountains are active volcanos, some of which form the wonders of the island.

Where "Wild Men of Borneo" Live.

Batavia, the capital and principal seaport, is reached by boat from Singapore for $22.50 first class. It has a population of 9,000 Europeans, 100,000 Javanese, 29,000 Chinese, and 2,000 Arabs. It is the starting point of the network of good roads (built by the English) that traverse the island.

I was told that Java's resources as regards objects of interest and means of enjoyment would last one for several months. There is big game handy for the sportsman; Hindoo temples for the student of ancient architecture and civilizations; primitive customs to be investigated by the socially curious; a model government system for the observation of the political economist; a chain of unrivalled volcanos to delight the geologist and scientist; famous botanical gardens for the botanist; and scenery of unsurpassable beauty and grandeur for the motorcyclist. So much have I heard Java praised, in fact, that I have determined to motor through it at the first opportunity.

Java is also a veritable gold mine for the Dutch, producing, as it does each year, 3,000,000,000 pounds of sugar, 35,000,000 pounds of coffee, 92,000,000 pounds of tobacco, 28,000,000 pounds of tea, 3,000,000 pounds of cocoa, and $2,000,000 worth of wood. Indeed, the English are still mighty sorry they ever swapped it for Ceylon.

Borneo is still partly British (Serawak and North Borneo), but three-fourths of the islands belongs to Holland. Although its area is greater than that of France, it is but little opened up, except in Serawak, and a tour through the island would be impossible. Besides, the noted "wild men" are still very real and very active.

No More the Chinese Queue.

The Philippines lie just north of Borneo, reached by boat from Hong Kong or the United States direct, and Luzon, the largest of their 2,000 islands, is covered with good roads and well worth visiting. Manila is now a busy American city, and American motorcycles feel very much at home here.

Finding it impossible, as I had expected, to motor from Singapore to Hong Kong, I continued with the "Bulow" four days more to this "Land of Sweet Waters," as the Chinese call it. The island of Hong Kong, about 10 miles long and three and one-half wide, lying just off the coast of South China to the east of Canton, where the earliest intercourse was held with China in 1625, was ceded to England by the treaty of 1841. Since then Hong Kong island and its city, whose real name is Victoria, has been rapidly developed as a British port, until now the great commerce of its splendid harbour, well sheltered from typhoons, is equalled by few other ports in the world.

The cosmopolitan city is built upon the slopes of a great peak (Mt. Victoria, 1,800 feet high), whose rugged, craggy skyline first caught my eye when approaching from the south. This, with the peak railway leading downward past the scores of big hotels and apartment houses nestling on the verdure-clad slope, and the miles of granite-faced commercial buildings lining the shore just back of scores of great steamers, completed my first view of China. And when I landed, the queue-less natives and modern shops abruptly reversed my idea of what the Orient was like.

CHAPTER XVIII
Clancy Investigates Chinese Conditions

Globe-Girdling American Rider Finds That He Cannot "Motorcycle" from Hong Kong to Shanghai

A s a people, the Chinese impressed me very favourably. They were quiet, respectful, courteous, and neat. All the ladies wore very becoming silk pantaloons, long, embroidered coats, and neat slippers, and far surpass the Japanese women, I found later, in attractiveness. Their hair is worn down the back in a simple braid, with long bangs in front, and is invariably straight and black. Several of them carried chubby, doll-like babies, with legs a-straddle their side or waists, and all seemed happy and well.

Southern China Is Without Roads.

I had hoped to motor from Hong Kong up to Shanghai—1,000 miles—and was much surprised to find that not only is there no road, but no railroad between these two cities. I was informed, in fact, that there are no roads in South China at all—except for a few miles outside of each large city. Canals, rivers, and the sea provide the only highways, except for the universal Chinese wheelbarrow— but I found there were even no trunk wheelbarrow tracks, else I would have surely attempted them. Touring cars and motorcycles are therefore as useless here as an aeroplane in a coal mine. I couldn't even have motored up to Canton—30 miles away. "Hong Kong can't be a bit typical of China," I thought to myself, and, indeed, it isn't, for with a few exceptions this great country, tremendously rich in mines and agricultural land, is still as far behind the times as it was 300 years ago. Certain it is that the "loan" could be well spent here. I had no choice, therefore, but to continue with the boat to Shanghai, and to make another try to get inland from there.

CONVENTIONAL TRANSPORTATION FACILITIES IN CHINA.

A couple of American marines from the United States gunboat "Wilmington," always standing in the harbour, showed me around the city that evening, and filled me full of hair-raising tales of their experiences in the recent revolution. But the most curious things I saw were two men sleeping on the floor of their shop with square wooden blocks for pillows, three joss sticks burning outside a modern doorway "to ward off evil spirits," they said, and a poor boy asleep on the sidewalk, crouching on his heels.

Gone is the "Chink" of Yesteryear.

During the revolution an imperial edict was issued compelling every man to cut off his queue. As the edict was not obeyed, soldiers were ordered to enforce it. Then street by street was blocked up and rich and poor alike clipped unmercifully. I wondered at first what became of all the queues, but, of course, each Chinaman keeps his own as his most precious possession. Some of them still wear the detached queue coiled up and pinned to his head, but the real old picturesque Chinaman is gone.

The bad weather continued, and as we went north cold set in as well; for both of which I was totally unprepared. At the upper end of the Formosa Channel the Island of Formosa (now belonging to Japan) came into view for an hour, but the rough sea allowed only a few passengers to be interested in it. Hugging the barren China coast, we arrived in the mouth of the broad and muddy Yangtsze River the third morning. Here a pilot came aboard to steer us up the Woosung River across the "heaven sent bar," and then up the Huangpa river to the anchorage opposite the great Standard Oil tanks, five miles below the city, at noon.

Shanghai, a City of the Present.

The entire country for miles around Shanghai (meaning "Approaching the Sea") is flat, and all the morning we had been floating past part of the vast plain of extraordinary fertility which has been formed by the ceaseless deposits of the Yangtsze River. The city of Quinsan, now 80 miles inland, was the seaport of this district 2,000 years ago. But the Yangtsze mud steadily encroached upon the sea, and will continue to do so as long as the river exists. This great waterway is navigable for 1,600 miles from its mouth, and through its course and that of the Grand Canal Shanghai is connected with the great emporia of the interior, most of whose produce pours into Shanghai, which is also the distributing center of an immense agricultural area. The oriental architecture of the picturesque farm houses, surrounded with spic and span gardens, which lined the banks, gave a true Chinese atmosphere to the whole country.

Shanghai was captured by the British during the first China war, in 1842. Since that time it has been made an "international settlement," having a separately owned American, English French, German, and native town. Coming up the river on the steam tender that met the "Bulow" at its anchorage, I was struck by the evidences of industry on both sides. Cotton and paper mills, ship-building yards, water-works, petroleum reservoirs, vast godowns and junks, filled with merchandise, length upon length of substantial wharves, and numerous lorchas, sampans, and swift steam launches, belonging to the many battleships and cruisers—American, French, English, Japanese, German, and Chinese—that were anchored in the stream; all giving evidence to the fact that Shanghai is the principal business port of the Far East.

Early Impressions of China.

Upon approaching the city, a row of lofty modern buildings overlooking the shady "Bund," or street that circles the wharves just beyond the Public Gardens, formed an imposing picture. The American Consulate, on our right, welcomed me with the Stars and Stripes flying from a tall masthead (with those on the battleships, the first specimen of my country's ensign that I had seen since leaving home), and soon I was the prey of a crowd of rickshaw coolies, who pulled those neat rubber-tired vehicles everywhere.

ROADSIDE RESTING PLACE FOR CHINESE "TOURISTS"

It happened to be Sunday, so I had to postpone my planned visit to the Consul, and spent the afternoon exploring the city with an English missionary bound for Japan. Selecting two rickshaws, we rode out Nanking Road, the principal thoroughfare of the Settlement, past scores of wide open business establishments—for the Chinaman has no Sunday—past hundreds of real Chinese wheelbarrows carrying everything from live pigs to people on their balanced racks, one motorcycle, several motor cars and many carriages filled with families of the aristocratically-inclined Chinese. Not a European was in sight.

Continuing past the Race Course, Cricket and Golf clubs, and Swimming Baths, where homesick Europeans distract their minds, we came to the lovely "Bubbling-Well Road." This street, rambling for two and one-half miles out into the country, we discovered to be lined with the principal residences in Shanghai, and they were beautiful places. At its end we found the Bubbling Well itself—far famed in Chinese annals, but now only a dirty, bubbling tank surrounded by a low stone railing. The two temples opposite, which we explored carefully, were much more interesting, and I snapped three pictures of them, but, as usual, it was too cloudy for great success. Returning by a different route, we came to Foochow Road, known as the "Paris of China." Here we found the largest and gaudiest eating houses, the finest fitted-up theatres in China, beautiful tea-houses, and shops of all sizes, where could be bought almost everything native and foreign; but not a suit of heavy clothes, which I needed badly.

We patronized one of the tea-houses and were horrified to have tea served in a rank imitation of the European style instead of Chinese fashion, as we expected. And that is one trouble with the Chinese. In their haste to adopt American or European customs, they follow every example they see, not stopping to discriminate, or to realize that some of their customs are better than ours.

The street below the balcony on which we sat made me wish for a moving picture camera, so fascinating was its ever fresh scene and changing players. One thing that impressed me was the fact that Chinamen seem to have no "typical" faces. Except for their color and eyes, the characteristics of all nations were represented in their physiognomy. They were quite different from the Hong Kong Chinese and spoke a different language. In fact, there are some 28 dialects in Chinese spoken throughout the country, and all are so different that even a Chinaman is "lost" a few miles from home. This lack of a unified language has been one of the reasons why the country has had so little internal development and commerce, and why it has been so difficult to govern. The new republican government, whose striped flag now flies on all public buildings, has already started to establish a common dialect, and in other ways is trying to render itself popular with the people as a whole.

YANGSTE OR MUDDY RIVER.

At six o'clock we attended evening service at the Church of England's Cathedral, a surprisingly fine building for the city, and later enjoyed dinner at the only good restaurant in the East, the "Carlton Grill," where an Hawaiian orchestra exhibited a long repertoire of American ragtime, which seems to be the only "popular" music there is; and I have heard it in every corner of the earth I have visited.

China No Place for Motorcycles.

A pouring rain drove us back to the ship that evening, and dark and early was the next morning when I arrived at the American

Consul's office. "You're in the wrong pew, if you came to China to motorcycle," he told me; "nothing but canals for a hundred miles around Shanghai. You can go a dozen miles west and get stuck in a rice field, but that's as far as you will go." "Aren't there any roads in the north of China?" I inquired. "Yes," he said, "from Peking there is one running north and one to the west, but they are almost impassable and lead nowhere but to a desert. Railroads are about as scarce as carriage roads, and more railroads will come before new roads do."

I felt like cursing for an hour, but soon became philosophical. "Give China a little time," I thought, "and she'll not only have plenty of trunk roads, but one of the richest countries on the globe. Nothing can top her." After that I decided to go on to Japan as soon as possible, and caught the same boat for Nagasaki. As she did not sail till the next morning, I had the whole day for exploration.

Even the Old Wall Is Coming Down.

Wishing to see the real China, or as she has been for thousands of years, I started off in a rickshaw for the native city, picking up a friend from the boat as I sped along. We found it had been surrounded by a wall about three miles in circumference, but that this old-fashioned institution is rapidly being torn down.

The streets are so low and narrow and winding that we were obliged to take a guide for 50 cents, a useful gentleman who spoke both French and English. First we followed a street about eight feet wide lined with one-story wooden shops without doors, windows or fronts at all, leading toward the center of the city. Most of the streets were much narrower and more confusing. Here were the booths of the ivory and sandalwood carvers, brass workers, fan makers, silk weavers and embroiderers, and porcelain shops. Here also were dozens of stores where nothing but ivory and bone dominoes were made and sold (for this is the favourite Chinese game with which they gamble). Further on we found scores of shops where celluloid ornaments were made up in imitation of jade. Everywhere were hand craftsmen energetically working on everything from tiny engravings to plaited baskets; the only machinery in evidence were Singer sewing machines, which, with Ford automobiles, Waterman pens, Eastman kodaks, and Gillette razors, are to be found in every city in the civilized world.

Where Nobility Smoked the Pipe.

Further on, numerous jewelry stores were very tempting, but the prices charged us were wholly unreasonable. The only way to shop here is to get a native to buy for you. Nearly every corner was adorned with a greasy, smoky, outdoor kitchen—the Chinese version of a quick-lunch—the strange food being kept hot in boiling fat.

Soon we came to the old city temple—400 years old—now used as a teahouse. This picturesque building stood on piles in the center of a small artificial pond, and was approached by two queer zig-zag bridges which are supposed to baffle the approach of evil spirits. The inside was full of smoke and grime, and dirty tea drinkers. It was the counterpart of an American saloon with alcohol absent. A Chinese doctor's shuttered house was next shown us; he was a genuine "medicine man."

A little later we came to a great iron door in a high wall. The latch string was not out, but some mysterious raps by our guide caused it to slowly swing back on its hinges, revealing a dried-up old man, and gaining us admission to the old Mandarin

Tea "Gardens of the East and West," and the club houses of those former rulers. Here was a treat for us indeed. First a cozy private temple of indeterminate religion appeared on our left. Opposite was the old orchestra pavilion, surrounded by small, blossoming peach trees. Following a winding circular path past queer limestone foundations, we came next to the opium house, looking just as it had when enhancing royal opium dreams but a few years ago. Now the guide called our attention to an archway decorated with minute figures carved in stone; then he pointed out the immense stone dragons that lay along the top of the walls, and next led past the dragon's pool of goldfish through several little tunnels up on a tiny knoll, where a summer house overlooked the whole enclosure. Entirely deserted though it was, the garden was so purely Oriental, so absolutely unique in every detail, that it would be impossible for a Western mind to conceive of it, or to originate any one of its countless weird yet here strangely beautiful designs. I would have liked to sit there half a day and dream.

Religion Hand in Hand With Fraud.

When we came to go out the door was locked, and the guardian demanded money. We gave him the equivalent of 15 cents each, but the rascal wanted more. Of course, my Savage was in my suitcase, or he would have changed his mind. Still, there were two of us to one of him, and finally he decided to let us through.

The Temple of Wenchang, dedicated to the God of Literature, was our next stopping place. The religion, a grand mixture of Confucianism, Tauism and Buddhism, was strangely served. Here the titular deities of the entire Chinese pantheon are represented by the most weird images and grotesque figures imaginable by the Oriental mind. There was a "joss" for every occupation—

merchants, sailors, soldiers, farmers, and business men. Josses to pray to before taking a sea voyage; josses for parents to beg man-children from, and josses for persons of every age from 12 years up—all were fierce and hideous. Before the principal ones were placed chicken, pork, and all kinds of choice cooked food which the god is supposed to eat. All the hundreds of them there appeared in the most grim and woebegone condition, though painted with enamel and gold, covered as they were by the soot from centuries of candle and joss-stick offerings, and the smoke of burnt "money" offered as a sacrifice. (The corrupt priests, as well as eating the josses' food, make worthless paper money, which they sell to the worshippers at par value for burning on the altar.) It was shocking, in fact, to find the grandest ideals of the human race so sadly mixed with present day chicanery and deceit.

Tobacco Is Succeeding Opium.

The worshippers were mostly women accompanied by small children, or very old women. Beggars seemed to prosper at the gates. Great barrel drums are used to beat an incessant tom-tom when service is held on festival days, as well as the three-toned, one-piece gong, and a great bronze bell which the guide also showed us.

Several other temples and shrines proved equally interesting, and before we knew it the afternoon had passed. Asking to be shown an opium den before we left, we were told that they have been entirely eliminated from the native city, but the guide knew of one shop-keeper in the French quarter who still smoked the drug, and we were fortunate enough to find him in full action. Lying on his side on a low couch, he held the stem of a curious long bamboo pipe in his mouth and the small opening of its mushroom-shaped bowl over the tiny tallow lamp, which was needed to keep the pipe going. He smoked rapidly, blowing all the smoke out of his nostrils, and stirring the opium in the pipe with a small wire until it was exhausted. He seemed a very healthy individual, full of business, and offered to let us smoke for 20 cents; but we were not sufficiently tempted. The fight against opium in China has been so successful that its use is now practically abolished. Tobacco is rapidly taking its place, cigarettes and finely shredded stuff smoked in a metal pipe with a bowl scarcely larger than a pea, are the most popular.

I liked the Chinese and their country, and regretted our short acquaintance.

CHAPTER XIX
"Nippon" Is a Fascinating Country

Many Quaint Scenes Are Afforded the
Motorcycle Tourist 'Round the World

I made no written notes on Japan and few mental ones, so preoccupied was my mind. But my observations in a general way are bound to be of value to anyone planning to motor in this delightful country. To me "Nippon," as the Japanese call their country, seemed the most fascinating country in which to motorcycle I have ever visited—everything is so different, so beautiful, so peculiar in its charm. The roads are good—except for occasional stretches—but there is a great lack of bridges across big rivers. Ferries are usually operated with some regularity, but delay always accompanies the appearance of a river. While the minor bridges are often too narrow and too weak for motor cars, they form no obstacle to the motorcycle. It is impossible to maintain an average speed of over 15 miles an hour, because of the numerous unprotected stone culverts placed in the road and not level with it, and because the roads are so narrow and full of right angle turns, which often hide a rickshaw or pony cart.

*TYPICAL VIEWS IN JAPAN, WHERE THE PEOPLE ARE
TAXED OVER ONE-FIFTH OF THEIR EARNINGS.*

While the people are very obliging, they are slow to get out of
the way. A horn does not mean "motorcycle!" to them, but "fried
fish," "pipes cleaned," or "clogs mended." The small, wiry horses
are generally quiet, but when their drivers jerk their mouths they
are apt to become much excited. One team broke its harness at

my approach, leaving a loaded cart of telephone poles squarely blocking the road.

Tokio a City of Disappointment.

The interior of the country is mountainous, but the coast road which I followed most of the way included few heavy grades and only one or two passes where special caution was necessary. I had hoped to reach Japan in time for cherry blossom season—usually extending from April 10 to 20—but, failing in this, I was delighted to find a large number of those beautiful trees, often as large as our apple trees, still in bloom in the high altitudes.

So neatly and closely cultivated was the entire stretch from Kobe to Tokio that I remember the whole of Japan as one great market garden, rice fields being in the majority. Each tiny tissue paper house, with its open second story front was also surrounded with a dainty garden and hedge, and never painted—the weathered wood blended perfectly with its setting. The whole of the time I was in Japan it was cold and cloudy. When I passed Mt. Fujiyama, about 30 miles west of Yokohama, I could see barely half way up its 12,400 feet of height. Only the graceful contour of the lower slopes of this "Peerless Mountain" were visible, but they formed an impressive background for the magnificent Lake Hakone. I was told that between 12,000 and 15,000 persons climb "Mt. Fuji" between July 15th and September 10th each season, and that the view from the top is indescribable.

Japan is crammed full of charming scenery, delightful tea houses half hidden in tree-sheltered nooks, quaint theatres and novel amusements, but its main attractions are undoubtedly its temples, palaces and treasures of Oriental art. Tokio was a disappointment. Although calling itself the "London of Japan," and boasting a population of 1,800,000, it has no public buildings of interest—except the Imperial Palace; has few buildings at all above one story, and is generally flat and uninteresting. In fact, all Japan is, architecturally, a bunch of temples and shanties, and politically nothing but a big bluff.

I want to urge all motorcyclists who plan an Oriental trip, however, not to miss Kamakura, near Yokohama, with its gigantic bronze statue of Diabutsu, wonderful temples, and rare works of art; Nagoya, the center of the cloisonné and porcelain industry of Japan, with its famous castle and two golden dolphins valued at 3,500,000 yen ($1,750,000); Nara, the art center of south Japan, where the old temples are truly architectural treasures; Kyoto, mentioned above (all on the way between Yokahama and Kobe), and, if possible, take in Nikko, about 90 miles north of Tokio, for it is said that the temples here present the climax of Japanese decorative and architectural art. The best roads and most beautiful scenery are to be found in the southern island, Kyushu, which with Hokkaido in the north presents to view curious old Japan still influenced by European civilization.

I saw no motorcycles, only one auto, and little of special interest at Yokohama, which gives the traveller who merely calls there no idea at all of the interior of the country. But its bazaars and shops are famous and especially good bargains in silk shirts and embroideries can be obtained if you care to do a little bargaining.

MT. FUJI, FRAMED BY SACRED ARCH.

MAJESTIC TOWER OF YASAKA.

Are the Japanese overrated?

My impressions of the Japanese as a people? Well, they are surely nothing to write home about. The men are all short on crazy wooden clogs, held on by strings squeezed between their big toes (these sandals are always left outside when they enter a house), and wear slovenly, quilted kimonos the whole day long. Sometimes you will see them in European dress, but more often only a derby hat or a cane is adopted to make them appear more ridiculous. I did not like the look in their eyes nor their mysterious manner. Although some were pleasant and jolly enough, I could not help feeling that they were not sincere—that they were trying to be diplomatic—that "seeming" meant more than "being" to them. Nor would I trust them around the corner with a sou. They all pretend to be very polite and bow to each awkwardly with their bodies stiff from their waists up, many times during ordinary conversation, and when one least expects it.

BRIDGE OVER THE GOJIO RIVER IN KYOTO.

The Japanese women are not so crafty. In fact, I saw some I could almost like. They are as short as the men and dress the same way—kimonos, sandals, no stockings, and queer, white, all cloth shoes, with a divided big toe and hooks at the heel. Many were plump and rosy but seldom graceful. Some were beautifully dressed in richly-designed kimonos, with blending color schemes, lovely sashes, and tasteful jewelry making them into life-size dolls; but none wore hats of any description, confining their beauty efforts to grotesque arrangements of their long, black hair. This hair dress takes so much time that it is done up but once a week, the women sleeping with their heads on a narrow wooden crotch to save it from damage. The women also smoke a long pipe with a metal bowl the size of a pea, and seem very fond of cigarettes.

STREET SCENE IN JAPAN.

English is spoken by merchants everywhere, road maps and gasoline charts can be obtained from the Japanese Tourist Office, The Welcome Society, or the Nippon Automobile Club—all of Tokio.

The men, women and the many chubby children seemed to be busy, well, and happy. It was hard to realize that they are taxed

22 per cent. of their earnings (the army being a terrible burden), or that Japan is a bankrupt nation. The California Alien Law excitement was at its height when I was there, and while I did not expect to have to use my Savage, I was on the lookout for trouble. It was extremely annoying to me to see a bunch of raw barbarians, as the majority of the Japanese are, bluffing Uncle Sam so successfully with their laughable threats of war! Upon my part I could not see how the Japanese could have the nerve to object to being refused land ownership in California, when they will permit no foreigner to own land in Japan. One Jap even admitted that his government's arrogance was all a bluff. The Jap army is huge, it is true, and could undoubtedly capture the Philippines and Hawaii, but Japan has no money to keep her soldiers in the field.

English is spoken with such surprising commonness throughout Japan that one would naturally mistake it for an American colony. This fact is but one which adds to the pleasure of motorcycling in this "Land of the Rising Sun." I am promising myself an extended tour throughout its entire length upon my 1914 Henderson.

Yokohama a Place of Temptation.

Yokohama is a splendid place to shop, especially if you have the folks at home in mind, and I could not resist the temptation to lay in a stock of silk shirts, at $1.50 per, for myself as well. Embroidery is also very cheap here, but one must not forget Uncle Sam's tax of 40 per cent, upon all such luxuries brought into the United States. When I caught the last launch for the "Persia" I strongly resembled a well-laden Christmas tree, and found it no easy job to stow the presents away cosily in my half of the tiny cabin that was to form my home for nearly three weeks.

The "Persia" itself was merely the size of a large steam yacht, carried four tall masts, and as a second class or "intermediate" boat of the Pacific Mail line, ranked as the smallest passenger carrying ship crossing the Pacific. Advertised as a "one class" boat, it nevertheless carried about 20 second-class and 100 steerage passengers. While $150 was charged for a first class passage on the "Persia" ($200 on the larger boats), second class rates totalled only half that sum. Figuring that there was no better way to earn $75 in 18 days than to save it, I took a chance on second class—but to my grief later.

To begin with, my cabin, sandwiched between two wards of the hospital, was just the size of a double bed square, and I had to share it with a 230-pound, 6½ foot Russian. My berth was laid directly over his on a level with two portholes. In the 3 x 7 foot space remaining we were compelled to wash, dress, keep our clothes, eat our meals, and spend most of our time. We were even so cramped that our door could not be opened until one of us stood up; and when our folding-shelf table was being "set," we both had to crawl into our bunks or go up on deck.

Interesting Fellow Passengers.

Luckily, the Russian was a very agreeable chap, turning out to be the son of a well-to-do Siberian mine owner, who was sending him to learn how to work his own mine at the University of California. At first he could speak scarcely a word of English, but after I had whiled away many a weary hour struggling with his limitations, we got so we could easily understand each other and play a number of card games. Toward the end of the voyage he would treat me occasionally to such delicacies as "All the woman are seasick," "I very like apple," "Very soon clouds is gone," "You are very many writing," "Oh, I finished speaking you." Finding him the picture of gloom one day, I inquired his trouble. "I do not happy," he replied. Being unable to refrain from laughing at his seasick plight, I aroused him to indignation. "I do not happy!" he emphatically repeated; "very soon I die. If I dead you are sorry, yes."

A grouchy Syrian, with his wife and three-year-old child, whom the father had already taught to smoke cigarettes, occupied the second cabin of our suite, and an 18-year-old Chinese boy and his girl wife, the third. This couple was scarcely less amusing than the Russian, the girl always appearing in fascinating light blue or black silk pantaloons and narrow embroidered slippers without stockings, and the boy doing his best to avoid our dog-like omnipresence. Observing his wife's unpopularity, I inquired in a brotherly manner (the Chinaman had spent three years in California) what was the matter. "You like being married?" "Not much!" came the quick answer; "wife too much trouble; always want go anywhere I go; always in way." "Why didn't you wait till you returned to the States and marry an American girl" I asked by way of experiment. But his reply was ready: "American girl spen' whole lot money. Chinee girl save, run good business, make store." In other words, a Chinese girl would make a better commercial partner. There seemed to be no initial love in the union; it was quite evident the young people's parents had arranged it all. Learning that the boy's father had recently died, I continued to be personal and asked the cause. "Oh, I guess he feel sick" was the reply.

All Alien Nations Are Left Behind.

Immediately after the anchor was hoisted, a thorough search was made for stowaways, the company's launch accompanying the ship for the first few miles to take back any that might be found. But none were discovered, so we soon faced out to sea in the teeth of a gathering storm. The southeasterly coast of the last alien nation I was to see before reaching the land of the Stars and Stripes remained visible for two hours and then sank.

Supper, served on a shelf in the hospital, as were all our meals until the first patient came, was ready at five o'clock and constituted the first big disappointment of the voyage. Tough meat, strong in more ways than one, almost raw potatoes, bread, bad butter, and tea strong enough to stand alone, completed the menu and formed a fair sample of what we had to exist upon for the next 18 days. There was no bullion in the foremoon, no afternoon tea. "Breakfast" occurred at 7 o'clock, and dinner—adding a lukewarm liquid "soup" to the thrice daily meat and potato (also cold from its journey from the galley up forward) arrived on our shelf at 11:30. We never had eggs or fish or ice cream, and only on Sundays and Thursdays were we offered dessert (a wretched pudding impossible to eat) and fruit. On these days also chicken replaced the constantly bad meat of the other days. Our only salvation were the apples and oranges that we were able to purchase at the first-class galley at the rate of "Two for five," and from which we obtained our chief sustenance.

CHAPTER XX
Clancy Once More on American Soil

**Leaves Golden Gate on Overland Journey
of 5,000 Miles Toward Home—Ascent of
Sierras Adds to the Rigors of the Trip**

erhaps the thing that impressed me most during my first day in San Francisco was the fact that everybody spoke English. It seemed almost sacrilege for the swarthy French waiters, the Italian fruit dealers, and the yellow Chinamen to be using my home language as their own.

ALLEN AND CLANCY BEFORE STARTING.

My Henderson was delayed in shipment from Yokohama for two weeks, but eventually it arrived on a Jap boat. I secured the bill of lading by waylaying the freight clerk as he disembarked, then hunted up a customs broker, trotted all over the town with him in a pouring rain, and finally, after a half day's wait, secured official permission to have my steed admitted to its native country and carted up to the Henderson agency in the city. The customs broker told me that he believed the United States customs regulations to be the most complicated of any country's, and I heartily agreed with him. Incidentally, he soaked me $3 for his services in addition to the $8 I had to pay for weight.

Across the Pacific Wrong Side Up.

The machine arrived wrong side up, and when I opened the box it became evident that it had ridden across the Pacific in that position. The oil I had neglected to drain from the crank case in my hurried departure from Yokohama had run down into the heads of the cylinders and so clogged things up generally that free use of "coal oil," as Westerners call kerosene, was required before I could get the engine running. All through this operation and the cleaning process that followed I had been continually aided by a most unusual youth from Los Angeles. Avowedly on a vacation tour with his 1913 Henderson, Robert Allen (they all called him "Bob") forgot his own interests completely in his unselfish endeavour to help me. Being much interested in my proposed trip across the continent, he soon became a very good friend; and finally, to my delight, I succeeded in inducing him to make the trip with me, at least as far as Chicago. Our route, laid out via Portland and Spokane, totalled just 5,000 miles, and was selected with the idea of charting a new northern transcontinental highway and to include Yellowstone Park.

ENCOUNTERING THE VICISSITUDES
OF AN AMERICAN "HIGHWAY"

Equipped with Plummer's "desert water bags," a small fibre trunk, Prest-O-Lite tank, and flying big San Francisco banners, we gaily sailed eastward from the city about five o'clock on the afternoon of June 2nd, on the huge automobile ferry plying to Oakland. Here an escort of local enthusiasts met us and guided us for the first 30 miles on our way to Sacramento. From here on we relied upon the small map books the Monarch Oil Co. gets out for California, Oregon, and Washington, as sign posts even here were few and far between. Although I had spent two days hunting for accurate road information in San Francisco, my inquiries had been profitless. Even the secretary of the American Automobile Association, although well acquainted with the good roads of Southern California, displayed dense ignorance—as we found later—of road conditions in the northern half of the State, when he told me that there were only 40 miles of poor roads on the whole 900 miles between San Francisco and Portland. If he had said there are only 40 miles of good roads he would have come much nearer the truth.

Sacramento Failed to Enthuse.

We spent the first night in the ranch town of Tracy, about 60 miles out, passed through the smart city of Stockton about noon the next day, stopping only for gasoline (selling at the dirt cheap—in my eyes—price of 20 cents a gallon) and an ice cream soda for lunch, and pulled into Sacramento by half-past three. A hard driveway encircled the beautiful capitol, so we rode around twice before halting for a photograph. Being "special sales agents" for the excellent back rests (Friel's) which we attached to our saddles before leaving the coast, we then made a tour of all the motorcycle shops in town (for Sacramento, like San Francisco, swarms with motorcycles) to demonstrate our wares. In vain, however; not a single dealer was live enough to put in a sample. "Sacramento always has and always will be dead," they'll tell you in San Francisco, and they sure are right! The heat was terrific here, and it hadn't rained for two months, so perhaps the natives have just cause for their sleepiness. We aroused one dealer enough to have him challenge us to a hill-climb contest the following morning, however, and in spite of the delay we took him up. Accompanied by a half dozen sporting sceptics, we wheeled out two miles beyond the city to the pet test hill of the town—up the side of a lofty railroad embankment (for there are no real hills in the whole district) with a 35 per cent grade. A rock pile made a running start impossible, so the test was to climb the grade without one. The dealer urged his well-known twin up the roof-like incline twice, only to get stuck near the top. Then came my turn. Whispering in the old boy's ear to do his best, I sallied forth and succeeded not only in riding to the top without great difficulty but in continuing on up the added grade and over the railroad track. Having established the supremacy of the "four" (and that a four" with 14,000 miles in its bones) over the "twin" forever, in the eyes of all present, we gracefully withdrew and continued on our way to the north.

NORTHERN CALIFORNIA'S "RENOWNED"
PACIFIC HIGHWAY—MERELY A TRAIL.

Assistance and More "Information."

A 20-mile stretch of deep sand now provided the first serious road obstacle we had struck. One of the many resulting falls broke the bolts holding my magneto distributor and lost us an hour before it could be wired on satisfactorily. The unmarked forks of roads and thick dust from numerous prairie schooners or emigrant wagons added to our delay. In the afternoon harder roads were encountered, which constantly sidestepped a mile or so to get around the square of a sheep ranch. We secured a fill of gas and our customary ice cream at Marysville, stopped for supper in the placer mining town of Oroville, and reached our night's resting place—Chico—before dark. We had already formed the habit of riding up and down the principal streets of the all-night towns in search of the largest motorcycle shop and to get a good idea of the village; and tonight we were fortunate enough to be able to ride up an inclined board right into the shop of a courteous mechanic, shocking him cruelly with our sudden appearance. He worked all the evening fitting bolts for my distributor, however, and bubbled over with copious, but erroneous, road information. By now we were well seated in our habit of eating only at lunch counters and avoiding hotels wherever a "rooms" sign could be found and often were supplied with a good double bed for 75 cents, or "six bits," in the lingo of the West. A "quarter" is an unknown animal out here, being always recognized by the title "to bits"; likewise 50 cents if "four bits," yet there is no such thing as "one bit."

BLACK BUTTES NEAR MT. SHASTA.

Up to now the whole State, with the exception of a few hills just out of Oakland, had been as flat as a pancake, and I began to long for some relief from the monotony. "You'll get all the mountains you want soon enough," remarked Bob, and he was more of a prophet than I thought. Long before we reached Redding, early that same afternoon, the southern ridges of the Sierras began to tower in the distance, and now we were about to enter that "40-mile stretch" of the road that was called bad. As the fair-to-poor roads we had been following had been called good, we expected the worst to come—and it came; but we were ready for it. Stopping off at the Redding express office, we removed our 50-pound boxes and shipped them on to Portland. Continuing to a store marked "General Merchandise," we purchased a cheap blanket apiece, and then waited long enough at a harness shop for the proprietor to sew up some canvas saddle bags to hold the few essentials we still retained. Next we tanked up with ice cream for ourselves, gas and Mobiloil for our Hendersons, and started off into the mountains at 3:40.

Roads That Were Wrongly Named.

Soon we had to employ a ferry for two bits to take us across the Sacramento River, and then climbed up an endless succession of long rocky grades full of exceedingly sharp corners and slid down the washed-out opposite sides for the rest of the day. It sounds lovely to read about it, but oh! how happy we would have been to have had two or three of those boastful boulevard riders that we met in every town along with us that day and those several that followed! Almost every sharp descent on the precipitous mountain sides would end in a tiny boulder-strewn lake. In this treacherous ford we would have to make a hairpin turn and shoot up an equally sharp ascent with enough speed to enable us to gain the top. Often we would meet turns half way up a mile-long grade of such sharpness that we could not make them at all. Having dismounted and gained the turn, we would have to run alongside our machines in exhausting installments until we reached the top, for the average of 22 per cent. grade rarely permitted us to gain enough momentum for riding again, once a curve had stopped our first rush or a washout thrown us down. Several of the descents were most dangerous and thrilling in the extreme.

It was about 5:30 that afternoon, when we came scraping down a long, sinuous descent so steep that we had to drag our rear tires, that we suddenly came upon a big Cadillac roadster stuck upon the outside edge of the road with a big stump between its front and back wheels. We stopped to offer our assistance to the discouraged looking driver and his young wife, who sat under a bush by the roadside combing her hair, and were welcomed like the sunshine in Ireland. We found that he had backed upon the stump when trying to avoid the frightened horse of a carriage that had passed an hour before, but that his worst trouble was the fact that his gasoline was so low that it would not run up the hill to his carburetter. He had already made a pilgrimage to a house in the valley below and secured a five-gallon can of kerosene, the contents of which he was now pouring into his tank with the hope that it would float the gas high enough to be useful; but the experiment soon proved to be a failure.

"Blowing" Motorist Out of a Hole.

We spared him a gallon and a half of the precious fluid in our tanks; but no matter how industriously his electric starter cranked that engine, it refused to start. I was in favour of rigging up a temporary auxiliary tank up near the radiator with one of the cans, but before we were driven to this expedient Bob had solved the problem. Removing the cap to the gasoline tank, he fitted his face into the bung hole and blew until he was red as a beet; then he signalled to the motorist to start the electric cranker, and blew some more. Pretty soon the engine spluttered away—and started, running until well warmed up. A repetition of the process of my self-sacrificing comrade started the motor again; this time the strong suction of the cylinders made the flow permanent and enabled the machine to gain a more level spot above. We refused the money offered for our gasoline, but were very glad to get a portion of the overstocked lunch materials these two grateful Klamath Falls people had brought with them from home. Six raw eggs, a small can of baked beans, a tiny can of condensed cream, a little bread, enough sugar and coffee for one meal, and an old pail to make it in, constituted the reward for our services. It was now getting dark and our motor friends had told us we were still in the heart of the mountains, so we had not gone far before we camped for the night by the side of a crystal stream. While I boiled the eggs and coffee, Bob laid a bed of weeds and leaves between our protecting machines; and, with our satisfying supper over, we stretched ourselves out in our blankets for the night. Several hours passed before we fell into a sound sleep, the strange voices of the woods whispered so loud, and the threatening lightning flashed so brightly; yet unconsciousness came at last, and gray dawn at its heels, all too soon.

Free Ferry Has Its Disadvantages.

Five o'clock saw us on our strenuous way again, breakfastless, with all the difficulties of the previous day accentuated fourfold. After an hour's struggle we slid slowly down a terrible grade that I defy any motorcycle to carry a man up, to the swift and turbulent Pitt River. Here a free ferry, operated solely by the force of the current, carried us across in a hurry and hit the other side with such a bump that both our machines were thrown to the floor, and Bob's lamp glass smashed. A stiff grade full of rocks headed straight for the top of the mountain on the other side, and soon I was stuck half way to the apparent top of it with a slipping clutch. Investigation revealed it to be dry as a bone, and by the time I had drained new oil from my tank and greased each plate, the broiling sun had cooked me to a turn. Now the sharpness of the ascent made riding impossible, and nothing remained but to let the machine pull itself up by degrees, I running alongside until too exhausted to hold it erect, and then resting until I had recuperated sufficiently to try it again. It took 20 rushes and two sweltering hours to get to the summit, more dead than alive; but that was only one hill. There were a full dozen even worse that had to be climbed that one morning, and we did not get a thing to eat till one o'clock. Bob's 8-horsepower and newer clutch carried him up most of the hills without special difficulty; but my compression was scarcely at its best on those sizzling grades—nor could I get my well-worn clutch plates and weak springs to hold with any adjustment. The result was that I had to take it out on myself, and if ever a man was bitter against motorcycling, it was I and then. Wild with the heat and exhaustion, I had come very near casting myself over the rocks in despair, when a kindly missionary caught up with a two-horse team and offered to tow me to the top of the last grade upon which my clutch had left me stranded. Even then I was so exhausted for lack of food and water that I could scarcely hold the machine erect.

FORDING IN CALIFORNIA.

At the top sat Bob, cool and collected and full of wild strawberries; never before have I envied anyone as I did my partner with his 1913 machine. Upon the second mountain side after that I again had to wait for the missionary; but after that I did not see him until we had finished our combination breakfast-lunch at a farm house hotel five miles further on.

Rocky Travel Amid Sylvan Scenes.

All through the mountains we had been regaled with the wildest and most rugged scenery. Silvery streams traced themselves far down in the rocky ravines along whose upper edge we rolled so perilously, a mad jumble of forest-clad summits stretched away to the horizon from every point of vantage, while along our trail (for trail was all the renowned "Pacific Highway" which we had been following so faithfully could honestly have been called any of that time) threaded its way between giant fir and hemlock trunks of a virgin wood.

Cooled off during lunch time, my clutch held bravely to the top of the next long grade, and from here on six miles of fairly good road cheered us with the hope that the worst was over. Yet soon we were plowing through countless fords, washouts, rock piles, and mud holes again, and around the wickedest of hairpin turns. Before dark we had reached the foot of "Castle Rocks," flatteringly reproduced in railroad folders, and by nightfall arrived in the combination summer resort and lumbering town of Dunsmuir.

Too stiff to move a muscle without pain, we awoke at nine o'clock the following morning devoid of the slightest ambition to make a transcontinental motorcycle tour. Among the crowd still gathered about our machines in front we found a tourist who had just arrived from Chicago on a one-cylinder "X," and we fully believed his assertion that he had "walked most of the way," especially as he had taken four months to make the trip. As far as we could learn, we were the first motorcyclists to have motored to Dunsmuir from San Francisco, and when we reached Portland we were told that no motorcycle had ever made the complete tour between the two cities before.

CHAPTER XXI
Resuming the Tale of Globe-Girdler Clancy

<hr>

Danger and Vicissitudes Encountered in Ride Through Central Oregon

After the parched, dusty ranches of California, the verdant farm lands and thriving orchards of Southern Oregon seemed most fresh and attractive. As famous for plentiful rain as its sister State is for sunshine, Oregon, and especially Jackson and Josephine counties, also is a land of torrential streams, snow-fed from towering verdure-clad, snow-hooded mountains; primeval parks, rivers, rivulets, nooks, and glens. Consequently, these two southern counties abound in bear and deer, pheasant, partridges, quail and wild pigeons, mountain trout, salmon and all things alive that delight the sportsman's heart and invite him to slaughter.

WHERE THE COLUMBIA RIVER ROAD WAS ABOVE WATER.

Trouble Often and Danger Everywhere.

Good roads led us north through clear air to Medford, which we discovered to be a city of vigorous growth, modern, and the outfitting center for tourists visiting Crater Lake National Park, 85 miles eastward, and the Marble Halls of the Siskiyous (great caves that penetrate a spur of the mountains for miles underground and duplicate many times over the wonders of the famous Mammoth Cave of Kentucky).

AT THE FOOT OF "BLACK BUTTE," NEAR MT. SHASTA, CAL.

The Rogue River Valley, sometimes termed the "Gateway to the Scenic Paradise of the Pacific Northwest," directed our way through an enchanting country, on to within six miles of Grant's Pass. Here I was riding along a grass-obscured footpath to avoid a sandy stretch of road when my front wheel suddenly dropped into a mean drainage ditch with force enough to crack the lower head ball-cup and lock the handle bars from turning. Over an hour was consumed in its removal, and the bending of a long bolt into circular form to take its place, enabling me finally to reach Grant's Pass at slow speed. A bicycle mechanic here was persuaded to spend the evening fitting up a substitute until a new part could be secured.

"Grant's Pass to Roseburg, 77 miles, a day of trouble." This is the way the following 24 hours were summarized in my diary. Soon after our seven o'clock start one of my clutch screws worked loose, caught on the adjustment bar, and locked the rear wheel with distracting suddenness. Soon after, some long, fearful grades overcame our lack of a "two-speed" and necessitated progress in installments; and by 12 o'clock we had covered only 18 miles. We overtook a prairie schooner, however, drawn by two blind mules, and escorted up the villainous hills by its owner, his wife, small boy, and dog. "Prospecting for work," the man informed us of his mission in the wilds. All his worldly goods were with him; brook trout formed his family's main sustenance, roadside grass fed his mules, and whether work for himself and his mules was encountered before he reached Canada mattered little.

The road climbed up a wilderness of scraggy hills, covered with spruce thinned by the ravages of many a forest fire, which left stricken, spectre-like, ghostly trunks scattered all around, only to tumble headlong down the steepest part of the other side. While resting on the tops we picked wild strawberries and attempted photos.

"WORLD TOURIST" IN PORTLAND, ORE.

At Wolf Creek village I took the lower road north (Bob having gone on over the hill to the left) and lost my way—also my gas tank cap. Eventually I found a sign reading "Roseburg 43 miles" and followed its direction up over a three-mile hill, to plunge down a switchback road of almost unbelievable steepness on the precipitous other side. At the bottom the road suddenly ended on the edge of a 200-foot width of the placid Wolf Creek. Luckily it had not rained for a couple of days, so the depth of the water never exceeded two feet. On the other side I came upon Bob's tracks again and in an hour more caught up with him plodding along at a slow rate with a broken fork, in the infernal Cow Creek Canyon.

Riding in a "Continuous Pigpen."

His two splinters of wood were soon replaced by my flat spark plug wrench securely wired on, and with this makeshift we continued over the nastiest thoroughfare either of us had ever seen, 38 miles more before night. In all the world I believe the 12 mile passage of Cow Creek Canyon constitutes the limit of road badness. No selection of words could even hint at the concentration of misery lurking here. Imagine a continuous pigpen two feet deep and frozen stiff, except where deep pools of water flooded it, or stretches of mislaid awkward logs bridged it cross wise in corduroy fashion; border it with two great twisting ruts varying from one to two and a half feet in depth; trim it with a scattering of great stones; vary it with gorge-like washouts and a few roof-like grades, and you have—only a smell of what the "road" in Cow Creek Canyon was like. The wonder of it was that my forks were not cracked, too, and that both of our frames and our motors stood the awful strain.

Only Bad Roads Over Steep Hills.

Arriving at Roseburg at 8:05, exhausted and starved from our lunchless day, we steered for the first "Eat" sign we could find, and soon the usual crowd had collected about our machines. After satisfying the inner man, we rescued our Hendersons from the gathering and piloted them to the nearest garage, where I found that my gloves had proven an irresistible attraction to some one in the crowd. As they were the seventh pair I had lost on the trip, I concluded to swear off wearing them. But I had to invest in a heavy pair of miner's shoes the next morning, while Bob's fork was being braized, to replace the new ones that had given away to the strain of fords, mud and rocks encountered since we left Sacramento.

TYPICAL "HIGHWAY" IN CENTRAL OREGON.

Soon after, I secured an order and deposit for two Hendersons in return for the territory of Douglass country, from the largest hardware dealer in town. He knew the nature of the roads we had come over, and said that if our machines could come up from San

Francisco and still be in such good condition as ours were, that he was the man who could sell them.

Two terrible hills were waiting in ambush for us just beyond the city that afternoon and soon the anguish of history was repeating itself. I got stuck in the middle of the second on a 30 per cent. graded stretch of corduroy. Before I could dismount and let my stand down to keep the machine from rolling back, Bob came rushing up at full speed, hit the full height of a log with a bang, just barely missed me, and got stuck 40 feet ahead. So steep and long was the hill that it took us an hour to get up the remainder of it. The rest of the day was "more of the same," including, in Pass Creek Canyon, a good imitation of the infamous Cow Creek which he had plodded through to the southward.

The poet would describe that afternoon's ride oh, far differently! He would say "Over the mountains and far away, into the deep balsam-scented woods, among the soughing pines, beside the murmuring mountain stream, along the crystal river's edge, through the silent places of Nature couched in the wildest grandeur of her lofty mountain fastnesses; among the haunts of the deer, the elk, and the cougar—all riotous in conception, alluring in imagination, but oh! how different from actuality, from our point of view!

True it was that the road did wind through forests of mighty hemlocks, firs, spruces and cedars—great giants that reared green spires heavenward 200 feet or more; that innumerable waterfalls splashed down from cliffs above into yawning chasms and ravines. Far below, dashing over the rocks and fallen logs, trout streams did sparkle in the sunlight and tempt our sporting blood. Of course, we skirted mountain sides on the level with green tips of firs whose roots were imbedded in the soil of the canyon 20 feet below. Yes, and here and there a rustic, rough-hewn logger's shack preceded a pretentious settlement, a busy mill marked the advance of commercialism, or a cleared valley and settler's homestead lent picturesqueness to the ever changing scene. But of these things we saw little. To us the winding, climbing, twisting, rock road was the all-engrossing subject; and, when riding, the concentration it required of us was absolute.

Down Hill Riding That Was Unpleasant.

Time and again, when dragging our rear wheels down the almost vertical hillsides, a stone would roll under our tires and lay us prostrate, sometimes pinned under the machine itself. When riding rapidly we were usually thrown clear of the machine in a fall. Going down hill it was common to get caught, and if either one of us were alone, and happened to fall on our face with the machine across our legs, it was a serious matter (considering that with luggage, Prest-O-Lite tank, spare parts, etc., they weighed 425 pounds) to get them off.

At Last a Stretch of Fair Road.

In spite of our troubles, we caught up with two Fords late that afternoon which had left Roseburg long before we did, and beat them into Cottage Grove to get gasoline. At least I did. Bob did not come along until half an hour later, and then he had a tale that excited my utmost sympathy. When riding along the side of a canyon five miles back he had accidentally opened his auxiliary air valve when he meant to close it entirely, and as a consequence had shot over the bank into the canyon below with amazing suddenness. Ten feet down the machine landed in a stout bush, and from this predicament he had been obliged to rescue himself and the machine, unaided. From Cottage Grove to the attractive city of Eugene, where we pulled in about 6:30, the road was fair; but although we had been following the "Pacific Highway" (to be) all of the time, it was the first stretch of even fair road we had met since leaving Medford.

CORDUROY ROAD WITH 30 PER CENT. GRADE.

That night it rained, hard, and continued to pour all the next day. From experience we knew it would be useless to try to proceed in the resulting slimy adobe mud, so had to camp there for the day. Only the discovery of a cordial Henderson agent and a good picture show consoled us for the loss of a day. During the night it cleared up a bit, and by 9:30 we decided to venture on—finding the mud, excepting in occasional hollows, had dried up with surprising quickness. We then proceeded, as one farmer expressed it, "like a bat out of hell."

Following the beautiful fresh valley of the Williamette River for 41 miles on its left bank, we crossed it into the typically clean little city of Albany, with asphalt streets and electric lights; filled up with gas and oil, and followed up the east side of the river into Salem. Here we rode out one of the many broad park-lined avenues to inspect the dignified Oregon State Capitol, and admire the beauty of the city in general, which is attractive in itself and ideally located from a scenic and agricultural standpoint in the luxuriant Williamette Valley. A smart shower reminded us forcefully of its moist climate, also, before we proceeded north at five o'clock.

Four Miles Only in Five Hours.

Indeed, it had rained more in the north than at Eugene, and although we had a friendly guide out of the city, we were soon struggling along a slimy, wooded road and suffering many torturing falls, one of which bent my handle bars exasperatingly. At dark we were still 15 miles below Portland, and instead of our troubles being nearly over, as we had hoped, the real tragedy of the day now began. Briefly, we struck a five-mile stretch of deep, sticky, slimy mud and it took us four hours to get through. Explicitly, those five miles were a nightmare of deep mud, ruts, falls, bruises, sweat, exhaustion, thumping hearts and misery. Our headlights only added to our difficulties, with their deceptive glare. "Oh, Oregon! What crimes are committed in thy name!" we exclaimed; to think that the main highway between the largest city and the capital of Oregon could be in such a condition!

With mudguards removed and strapped on our luggage, we eventually emerged from the slough of despond at 11 o'clock onto hard roads; and here we met a tourist on a twin bound over our route for Norfolk, Va. Finding him to be a rider of short experience, we urged him by no means to attempt to get through that mud stretch until morning, and advised him to make love to the hay-loft in a near-by barn, telling him we would do the same if our empty stomachs would permit us. Leaving him to "think it over," we continued on and at 11:30 rolled in upon the gala streets of Portland, only in time to see the crowds going home from the last night of the annual Rose Festival, which we had hurried all the way from San Francisco to see.

Portland, the City of Roses.

Called the "City of Roses," Portland is a rapidly growing city of over 200,000 population, set like a gem among hills of green, and backed by a line of no fewer than five snow-capped mountain peaks. Five days were consumed here, the first three in purchasing a new clothing outfit for me, leggings and all; having an extra 62-tooth sprocket milled out of a square piece of boiler plate to give my machine a low gear when needed in the mountains (with the Rockies in mind), and the last two in waiting in vain for the waters of the overflowed Columbia River to recede from the roads to the east.

CHAPTER XXII
Around the World Clancy's Oregon Struggles

~~~~

Swollen Streams and Mud Impede His Progress from Portland to Pendleton

One of our reasons for coming up to Portland had been the idea that the valley of the Columbia River would give us easy passage through the Cascade Mountains and avoid the strenuous crossing of the Sierras included in the central transcontinental road. En route, however, we had encountered in northern California grades and roads far worse than those we had so laboriously circumnavigated, and now we were doomed to another disillusion—the road along the Columbia was impassable!

Swollen Stream Made Road Unridable.

Our thorough search for information concerning other roads was, as usual, unfruitful. No one had even heard of an automobile making the complete trip between Portland and Spokane, Wash. —the next big center on our route—because even in the dry season the deep sand in the valley necessitates the shipping of the machine on the boat between Portland and The Dalles, 88 miles up the river. But now, the Columbia's flood was so great and so turbulent that even the river steamers could not get up beyond the locks, and to get out of town we were forced to express our machines to The Dalles and take the train. "Double merchandise" was the demand of the express rates, and by the time we had paid for our tickets in addition, we agreed that we were decidedly "out of luck."

WASCO, A TYPICAL COUNTRY TOWN IN THE EASTERN PART OF OREGON.

To compensate for part of this unexpected expense, Bob slept on a pile of burlap in one corner of the garage in The Dalles, where we stored our machines that night, while I courted Morpheus upon the back seat of a touring car—without much success.

All along our train ride up the river, we had been regaled with the grandest cliff and river scenery (considered by some to exceed that of the Hudson in beauty), and interested by grotesque-colored rock formations. For 15 miles more the next morning the majesty of the valley continued to expand, hinted at by the photographs reproduced here, and then it suddenly widened out into an unlovely desert waste—a wilderness of barren hills and steep gulches, through which we were compelled to pass for hundreds of miles.

The soft, hazy colors of the "Bad Lands" reminded me of Africa, but the cowboys we met along the road, and the cherries we "procured" at an occasional irrigated ranch were original in themselves; so, by the way, were the charges of 50 cents for a half-mile toll road, and another "four bits" to be ferried across a small tributary to the Columbia, a little further on. This ferryman not only had a monopoly on all the traffic through that country and charged what he liked, but he also maintained a pair of huge mules for the sole purpose of helping motor cars get up the famous John Day Hill (probably the steepest, longest, and wickedest in the State, which we scraped cautiously down on our way to his ferry) at the rate of from $15 to $20 a car.

AFTER ONE GOOD NIGHT'S SLEEP IN PORTLAND, ORE.

Now the rain, which had come down steadily all the while we were in Portland and had let up for only a day or so, started to pour again, turned the sandy roads into slimy mud, and held us down to nine miles more for the day.

Thirty-three Miles Through Mud.

A puncture delayed me a half hour when Bob was ahead, so by nightfall I was skidding along the dreary gulch all alone. Soon a young cloudburst made the road so slippery that my machine fell over nearly 20 feet, compelling me to give up the struggle. Abandoning it by the roadside, I started to walk ahead, hoping to find Bob waiting for me. A mile up the gulch I came upon a farm house and learned from the farmer that Bob had passed by long ago, but succeeded in getting the rustic to take his two mules down to tow my machine up to the house. That night I slept with the hired man.

The rain let up for a while the next morning and four miles further on I caught up to Bob, who had slept in a hayloft in a ramshackle barn that night and breakfasted on sardines and gingersnaps at a crossroads grocery.

Thirty-three miles was our total for that long day—a continuous exhausting struggle with the mud holes of the road following up Rock Creek. Two weeks before a cloud had burst somewhere up the river and caused a sudden flood to sweep down the valley, carry away $3,000 worth of stacked hay for one farmer, a part of another's house, overflow the road for days, and soak it into a mere track of slippery clay. It was through this mess that we floundered all day, falling continually onto the rocky bank to one side, into the bushes on the other, or into the mud pools themselves. The exertion of lifting my loaded machine up on its feet so often, aside from the pain of the falls, finally caused me to "see stars" from the strain. At one place we came upon some dead fish in the road, causing me to remark to Bob, "Pretty high water, to drown fish, eh?"

Even Africa Was Not Worse Than This.

My magneto distributor varied the excitement by chipping off a chunk inside which clogged up the gears, locked the shaft and caused no end of trouble. At the shack town of Olex, a three-mile 22 per cent. grade started its upward flight, so I clapped on by 62-tooth sprocket, lengthened my chain, and beat Bob to the top without trouble. Now a desolate plateau stretched out into the purple haze of the distance. Badger, ground squirrel and rabbit holes pepper-boxed the road with uncomfortable frequency, and often the wheel tracks along which we rode would multiply themselves into three parallel roads of equal poorness. Usually their centers and sides were so high with weeds that we looked to each other like magical pathfinders rolling through a field.

Once a mud pond (we usually managed to get around them) appeared unexpectedly when I was making a fair rate of speed. I started to skid in the middle of it and shot half way up a steep bank before the machine fell over—with me under it. Near Ione we struck our first straw roads—thick layers of straw laid across mud stretches to give the slime some body or texture—and they were some welcome! "We love asphalt, but oh you straw!" was our joyous cry that afternoon.

The flat ranch town of Ione was so flooded that we couldn't get out of it, but were so completely all in that we were not sorry to be compelled to seek shelter here for the night, tumbling early to bed aching all over. Despite the fact that I had become thoroughly accustomed to the hardships encountered during the long ride around the world, I actually suffered until sleep finally gave me a welcome relief.

For a wonder, it cleared off that night, enabling the roads to dry up a bit, and aiding us to make a total of 71 miles the next day into Pendleton. Numerous abrupt hills encouraged the frequent use of my low-speed sprocket, but for the most part the tracks were far too high for the clearance of a motor car. Frequently the weeds concealed large porcupine and coyote holes, into which our wheels would drop with painful suddenness, only to be thrown aside by the earth mound piled up beyond.

Wanted—a Few Ice Cream Sodas.

Fifteen miles west of the echoless town of Echo, we struck a veritable sage-brush of mesquite desert and had to fight our way through hot, deep sand till we got there. We discovered that sand is almost as bad as mud for letting your feet slip out from under you and the wheels slide away when you are trying to set your machine on its pegs for the twentieth time. But the thought of the ice cream sodas ahead at Echo cheered us on, and when we reached there it took two apiece to even slake our thirst.

Pendleton now lay 26 miles to the southeast, with no sand en route, according to the natives. We found plenty, however, but that was not the worst of it. I ran out of gasoline eight miles short of the town when Bob was a mile ahead. The only thing to do was to walk ahead a mile and a half till I found him waiting for me, send him back to pour some from his tank into mine via a Tuxedo can, and to trudge back again to get my "hoss." Soon after, we discovered we were both completely out of oil, but were fortunate to be able to graft some off a Ford that happened along just then; and in spite of all our troubles, rolled into the city of Pendleton before dark. "Let's go eat," said Bob, after we had put our machines to bed in a garage, and we did; taking in a picture show afterwards by way of celebration.

*VIEW OF PENDLETON FROM THE HILL
ROAD APPROACHING IT.*

*HIGHWAY OF MUD THAT'S CALLED A "ROAD"
ALONG ROCK CREEK, ORE.*

CHAPTER XXIII
Clancy Reaches Montana via the "Chimney"

~~~~~~~

Quagmire Roads of Oregon and Lumber Paths of Washington Prove Level by Comparison with Rock Strewn Precipices of Montana

About nine the next day we pulled out over good roads that didn't last long towards Walla Walla, Wash., only 47 miles north; but it took us all day to get there. Ten miles out we struck the rain belt again, and as it had rained harder here that week than it had for 40 years before, we were soon fighting our enemy "gumbo" again. I had had all I wanted of that kind of riding, and as we were following alongside a railroad track near a flag station, I determined to wait five hours for the afternoon train. Bob, however, chose to stick it out a while longer, and continued the fight, while I swapped lies with a friendly "bo" in a sidetracked box car. After an hour or so his restless spirit drove him away to "hit the ties" and leave me to philosophize alone.

Oregon Roads Too Much Quagmire.

After the weary hours had dragged themselves away, the train hove in sight down the track and I manfully flagged it with an old flour bag. At first the conductor refused to take my Henderson into the baggage car, but my pleadings soon took effect, and with the aid of the brakeman and an obliging passenger we boosted and heaved the awkward machine up the slight embankment and through the door of the car seven feet above the ground. I was mighty thankful when it was loaded, I tell you, especially when I saw the fearful roads that lay ahead.

IN THE MUD, FOURTH OF JULY CANYON.

At the second station, as I expected, there was Bob waiting on the platform, he, too, having been conquered by the mud. He joined me in the smoking car and the words we spoke were few and far between, as we rode through a great wheat country on to Walla Walla.

Walla Walla is about the slowest, sleepiest, deadest town of any pretensions that I have ever met. Its broad streets are lined with saloons, wherein the cattlemen and farmers of the surrounding ranches find their amusement, and were devoid of interest to us except for the huge cherries of the grocery stores in which we indulged to the extent of two pounds and 20 cents each.

Royal Reception Repaid Hardships.

After spending two nights here we were most joyful, therefore, to have the rain desist and to get away for Spokane. The roads of eastern Washington turned out to be far superior to those of Oregon, and the country much more attractive, being wooded with fir and spruce toward the north. The breaking of our record with a 156-mile day was the grandstand finish of the week of misery "between Portland and Spokane."

Spokane will always occupy a cozy corner in my heart, for it was here that I got my first taste of "Western hospitality"—and a good big taste, too, for Bob and I stayed here 12 days. Our first host was jolly Manager Lair of the Henderson agency, who welcomed us as kings, dined us in his own home, and rode us all over town on a tandem. His popular foreman, Fred Cedar, next took us and our machines in hand, and then we were turned loose among a wild bunch of rough-riders, for Spokane is a great four-cylinder town. Those boys certainly knew how to enjoy life, and we were kept going in a whirl of fishing parties, dinners, hill-climb contests, tandem jaunts, and theatre sieges until our "in training" habits were demoralized.

Spokane a Hard City to Leave.

As a city Spokane is a live one, too. I was awakened the morning after our arrival by a newspaper reporter, seeking to imbibe the story of my life from a pajama interview. Smart skyscrapers and asphalt streets substituted the overgrown lumber camp I had expected to see; and business activity seemed much more brisk than in Portland. Over 100,000 people, in fact, are enrolled upon the census of this city of steep hills, great waterfalls and good air, while all the young ladies of the city distinguished themselves by wearing low-heel shoes.

The week we planned to stay for recuperation purposes upon our arrival in Spokane stretched out a couple of days, and then a deluge of unseasonable rain imprisoned us here three days more. Our delightful visit finally ended, however, as all good things do, and with very meagre road information we set out to blaze a through route over the Cour d'Alene and Bitter Root Mountains to Missoula, and Butte, Mont. Fifteen miles east we passed over the Idaho state line, and immediately beyond the lovely lake of Cour d'Alene (big enough for a passenger steamer) we began to climb as long succession of the tremendous grades of the Cour d'Alene Mountains. My low-gear sprocket did excellent service here, but as Bob had nothing lower than 4½ to 1, I had plenty of opportunity to enjoy the view from the top of hills he had to conquer in installments. I felt much gratified to be able to turn the tables on him after my strenuous days in the Sierras.

FIRST NIGHT'S CAMP OUT OF SPOKANE.

Down in the Bowels of the Earth.

The first night out our supper consisted of stale bread, syrup, and water, seduced with difficulty from the hut of a telephone lineman's station, the only respectable habitation in the mountains; and when it got dark we spread our blankets inside the enclosure of a roofless cabin "of yesterday," dug a hole for our hips, and consigned ourselves to the mercy of the mosquitoes and timber rats.

For a wonder it did not rain that night, so after brewing a pail of powdered coffee over an unambitious fire in the morning, we continued on through the Fourth of July Canyon, famous for its infamous grades and poor roads—and now additionally wicked because of numerous mud holes—fostered by the shades of the tall timber, in many of which our machines stuck and stood alone without other support than the deep muck.

At the first little hamlet we breakfasted on nut chocolate and chemical "orangeade," and then continued over good roads to Kellogg, a mining town large enough to support a newspaper, the sole reporter for which interviewed us in detail as we tanked up with gasoline at 30 cents per gallon. A public-spirited citizen also added a Kellogg pennant with his compliments, to my rapidly growing handlebar collection of pennant souvenirs from each State and large city along our route.

Just before reaching Kellogg we came upon the famous Bunker Hill and Sullivan lead mines, and after finding that visitors are not permitted to enter the mine during the daytime we made a careful tour of the huge mill where the ore-rock from the mine is first crushed by great whirling maws into pebbles, then pounded and sieved into powder, and finally separated on great shaking water tables into a mixed lead and silver mud, which is sent to a foundry for the refining process.

THE BUNKER HILL, A TYPICAL LEAD
MINE IN KELLOGG, IDAHO.

Twelve miles more of good roads took us on to Wallace, Idaho, and the center of the region that was swept by a great forest fire two years ago at the cost of a hundred lives. Indeed, a blight seemed to have struck the whole country. Instead of being clad in fir and spruce, the surrounding mountains bristled with wrecked and whitened tree trunks, each one but a monument to some towering monarch that was withered by the ravishing flames, and together forming almost as desolate and lamentable a scene as a war-time graveyard.

By right, we should now also be in the center of the "Wild and Wooly West," but the white-shirted, tuxedo-clad garcon who waited upon us behind the lunch counter that noon, and the electric-lighted, paved streets of Wallace itself, confirmed our suspicions that the real wild and woolyness of the West is now to be found only in motion picture shows.

Learning that we desired to go down into a mine, the newspaper reporter who interviewed us here—happening to be a fraternity brother of mine—secured a letter of introduction for us to the superintendent of the Greenhill-Cleveland lead mine, seven miles up the canyon to the north, and soon we were off on this side trip, beating the railroad train up the grade by several minutes.

Luckily, the cordial superintendent was about to start an inspection tour of the mine, so we were soon astride a small electric locomotive riding through a hot, black hole straight into the heart of a mountain. Three thousand three hundred feet from the entrance, the tunnel suddenly widened out into an arched cavern, where the boilers and engines for operating the hoists and heating the compressed air for the automatic drills far down in the mine, were located. Here it was so hot that the men were clad in nothing but overalls, and the air so oppressive that I seemed to be suffocating and wished a hundred times that I had not come. Pretty soon the hoist raced up the shaft to dump its tons of ore-rock into the "skip-way." Under the bucket was a little platform car loaded with blackened and begrimed miners "changing shift," and soon we had taken their places under the deep bucket. "Fourteen," said our guide mysteriously to the hoist operator, and soon we were dropping noiselessly down 1,400 feet into the bowels of the earth. Every hundred feet a "level" flitted by with incredible swiftness, and before we knew it we were walking along the narrow track of level "14," one-quarter of a mile underground. It was little consolation to know that the shaft went down 800 feet further.

Viewing a Shored-Up Mountain.

Guided by an occasional electric bulb and the ray from the superintendent's acetylene lamp, we walked along the solid rock tunnel—dripping with water from mysterious springs—for 2,400 feet, to its end. The three compressed air trip-hammer drills at work here making holes a yard deep for blasting charges were absolutely deafening, and our stay would have been short had not the "boss" stopped the Slavs who were operating them while he pointed out the "ore leads" in the rock which they were following.

Then we climbed up after him into three of the timbered levels above and learned that the entire mountain, from the 22nd to the top level, where the ore had been taken out was braced against collapse by a lattice-work of great timbers.

Returning to the hoist, we inspected the two great electric pumps, each with a capacity of 1,500 gallons a minute, which keeps the mine free from water, and then were hoisted up the black shaft into the stuffy boiler chamber again. Taking no chances of losing the first train out, we joined the begrimed miners of many nationalities in the narrow cars, and soon were hauled out into free sunlight again, thankful enough that we had not been destined to be miners!

Two roads or trails led over the Bitter Root mountains to the west of Wallace, and each way had staunch advocates and equally emphatic haters. Few men in the town had been over either track personally, however, so we decided to take the shorter of the two to Missoula, Mont. via Mullen. A minute later an old woodsman informed us that owing to a recent cloudburst in the mountains, fallen logs now blocked this road in several places and that we could not get through, even on horseback. Having no choice left, we at once started off on the northern trail, 150 miles longer, and crossed two 4,000-foot summits into the old-time mining camp of Murray, 20 miles north, by nightfall.

HALF WAY UP THE MURRAY GRADE.

Like the Days of the "Old-Time West."

The ground being too wet and the weather too threatening to sleep out of doors, we decided to spend the night in the house of a noisy German woman, where we had supper and had been offered a room. Soon after we learned that our hostess and her assistant—solicitous "Minnie" White—had been the victims, but the night before, of a raid by two drunken lumbermen. In the course of the broil the "lady of the house" had been shot at several times and Minnie dragged by her heels from her bed and beaten. The sheriff had been held up and deprived of his "six-shooter" and the whole town terrorized by the same men, for whom the sheriff's posse was even now combing the hills.

We seemed to have run across a bit of the "woolly West" after all, we thought, and when the old lady pulled out a cigar and went to it, while Minnie rolled many and sundry "pills" for herself, we tumbled to the fact that we had also stumbled into a bit of "local (red) color." Still, that was the only establishment in the place where we could have had shelter at all, so we stayed on and enjoyed a good night's sleep, but winced at the outrageous bill of the morning.

The rain set in about 4 A. M. and we feared we were in for a long siege in this God-forsaken "dump," but it let up for a while soon after 9 o'clock, and we set out upon the hardest day's run of the entire trip.

After splashing through the mud holes and slipping around the turns of a grass-grown lumber road for six miles, we struck an eight-mile hill, and it took us four hours to get to the top. While we struggled up the slimy, stair-like path, which always seemed to go over the high spots instead of around them, a consecutive series of the most terrific thunderstorms on record swept up that precipitous valley with what well may be called a heartrending roar.

Resting between the laborious installments of our ascent, we became helpless spectators in a mighty battle of the elements, in which giant trees to the right and left fell splintered victims to stray lightning shafts, and newly-spilled cascades, blood of the clouds, gushed across our path.

Six Hours of Dangerous Progress.

We bore charmed lives, however, and gained the 5,000-foot summit of the ridge that forms the border line between the rugged states of Idaho and Montana, merely soaked and exhausted. The deathlike stillness that preceded the most tremendous blast of all, to withstand which we propped up our machines staunchly, found us also blasé to danger, for we merely threw ourselves on the saturated ground and let the wind wreak its fury on the trees.

WHERE MONTANA AND IDAHO MEET.

While it had taken us four hours to climb up that mountainous ridge, it took us six hours to get down the other side. We had expected to enter Montana by the back door, but hadn't planned to go down the chimney. The ascending trail in Idaho had been unspeakable, but the descending track, our first impression of Montana's roads, was barely passable for two tough mules and a light buggy. Crowded with sharply-edged rocks a foot or more in height, and so steep I had to put on my Weed chains to hold my locked rear wheel from dragging down too fast, scattered with misstrewn corduroy logs, and overflown with soft-bottomed pools of water throughout its six-mile slope, each and all the cause of numerous painful falls (17 upon my part that afternoon, and as many agonizing 375-pound lifts again, as well as several punctures).

The great wonder of it is that we ever got down alive at all, and with whole machines. The deep dents in the rims of our wheels, their broken spokes, and the bruised handlebars remained the only proof of the war we had been through—the only wounds of the cruel, jagged rocks we had pounded over, and the wretched holes we had fallen into.

When night fell I had not seen Bob, who was somewhere ahead, for an hour, and I could find no match to light my lamp. Floundering on in the darkness, another nasty fall bent my handle bars so badly I could barely balance the machine after I had used up my last ounce of strength in setting it up. So weak was I with the 10-hour lunchless strain that the next deep pool bowled me over again, and this time I had to sit down in the bushes and wait several minutes to gain strength to even drag my steed from the water, which its hot cylinders was fast turning to steam.

But on level ground again the trail improved, and eventually, at 8:45, I came upon Bob waiting at the door of a crude prospector's shack, and learned the blessed news that here we could have shelter for the night. Bob picked up and cared for my faithful

Henderson, which had fallen again from my nerveless grasp, while I staggered to the door to be welcomed by the cheery old miner, who already had supper nearly cooked for us. After a few minutes' rest by the stove, I recovered sufficiently to wash up, and later did justice to the fresh biscuit-bread, bacon, canned string beans and coffee feast the Good Samaritan miner had laid out for us.

In spite of our unbroken 12-hour struggle, we had covered only 20 miles that eventful day.

Guests of a Miner Samaritan.

Dishes over, we repaired to the other end of the long, narrow, one-story shack to sit about the heater and talk over current events, upon which Mr. Isam Cox—for that was the kind-hearted old prospector's name—seemed surprisingly well informed, until we became too sleepy for utterance, and then "turned in" upon the wide bunks built into the wall. The aged blackness of the pillows and covers did not worry us a bit, and the next thing we knew we were awakened by the miner's lusty cry "Change cars!" to find morning had come and breakfast was ready.

Filled with his coffee, bacon and biscuit bread, and rested on his couches, we had been, not boarders, and as guests an hour later to have our proffered payment for accommodation refused. Guests we had been, not boarders, and as guests we could simply promise him a copy of the photos we snapped of himself and his abode in the early morning light, before saying our good-byes and taking up our way down Prospect Creek.

Ten miles on muddy road led to the long, new bridge across the wide and turbulent Clark's Fork river and into the town where we had expected to get lunch the day before, Thompson Falls. Here we secured gas at 40 cents a gallon and ice cream at "two bits a fill," before starting off on a long detour through the Flathead Indian Reservation to get around a piece of road under reconstruction over an almost inconceivably rough trail that wrenched and wracked our machines and ourselves almost as savagely as we had been racked on the afternoon before.

CHAPTER XXIV
Clancy's Tour in Western Wilds

<hr>

**Globe-Girdler Finds Almost Impassable Roads
and Encounters Difficulty in Traveling "Northern
Route"—Mosquitoes and Stones the Bugbears**

Following up the green ribbon of Clark's Fork, on our way south to Missoula, through Horse Plains, we arrived at the settlement of Palermo in the late afternoon, purchased a can of baked beans and some crackers and cheese at the cross-roads grocery, before making our last two miles to the site of our night's camp, which we had planned for this the first pleasant day of the week. Stopping on a bluff commanding a glorious view of the winding river and mountains to the north, Bob built a fire and prepared supper while I made a pilgrimage down to the river in search of water to fill the misshapen tin pail I carried in my luggage bag. Supper eaten, and diaries written by the firelight, we spread the old awning we had purchased in Portland over our steeds, which had been placed side by side, then rolled up in our blankets, and with our back rests for pillows attempted to sleep. But the myriads of mosquitos which hummed around our heads all night like a swarm of bees and pounced upon any portion of nose or ear that happened to be exposed, made unconsciousness as remote as it was desirable, while the hard ground grew anything but chummy with our hips. In spite of the cold and those "we-neversleep" pests, we managed to get some rest, but rose at 5:30 to build a fire, finish up our provisions, take a snapshot of our camp, which we dubbed "Mosquito Lodge," and make an early getaway.

Obstacles Met at Frequent Intervals.

Soon we had to dismount to pass through two private gates that barred the road, and then began a long flight through bridgeless creeks, over impossible trails, over boulder-strewn hillsides fit only for the Indian ponies we saw picking their way through them, as directed by their brightly-costumed riders, and around flooded stretches of road, the whole morning long. Two rock-strewn rivers demanded our united strength to overcome the obstacles they offered to the passage of each of our machines.

ON A FIVE THOUSAND FOOT INCLINE.

The afternoon was merely a repetition of the morning's anguish, except for the fact that the Mission Range of the Rockies, snow-patched along their upper peaks, now towered in full view to the east, reminding me strongly of the Pyrenees. At 3 o'clock we pulled triumphant into Missoula, dirt-begrimed, but happy in our victory over 60 more miles of pioneer motorcycle road.

Where Every Third Man is Drunk.

Missoula surprised us in the aspect of a smart, modern near-city, with wide asphalt streets, public drinking fountains, and an elevator building. But after Bob's bad cold had delayed us here two days, we were glad to get away for Butte. Following the Northern Pacific Railroad up through Bonita, Drummond, Garrison, Deer Lodge, gradually climbing all the while, we managed to cover the 142 miles of frequently good roads in eight hours, and rolled into the rawest town I have ever visited—Butte, Montana—at 9 o'clock that night.

Our first impression of Butte, Mont., gained late one evening after a day's ride of 142 miles from Missoula, was anything but complimentary. In the first place, the main street was so steep, running up the sheer side of the copper mountain upon which the city is located, that there was no comfort in riding on it; second, few people seemed to be able to speak English and no one could direct us to a garage; third, policemen were nowhere to be found; and fourth, every third man seemed to be sadly drunk. By dint of careful search we finally found a garage, deposited our machines, and charged for the first lunch counter we could find, not having eaten since morning. The prices on the menu card were our first warning of the cost of living in Butte. Here, in this middle-class restaurant, they rivalled those of the best hotels in New York.

The cause of this condition we afterwards learned to be the fact that Butte is probably the strongest labor union town in the country, and as there is but one big industry—copper mining—in the city, practically all of the wage earners are organized in a miners' union and receive an average of $6 a day. The boys who are apprentices in the mines get a minimum of $2.50 a day, and plumbers will not fix a leak for less than $4—a half-day's pay. But the miners are no better off for this extraordinary wage scale, because the standard of living in Butte is proportionately high, the shop and restaurant keepers taking advantage of the situation.

Butte, an Unattractive City.

After a 10-hours sleep in a very ordinary but costly room, we discovered the next morning that Butte, although the largest city in Montana, is the most unattractive city either of us had ever visited. As the whole country for miles around is treeless and grassless, of course Butte is treely and grassless, too. Even in the business section the buildings are mostly very cheap both in architecture and appearance, and every block or two a towering derrick-hoist rears its awkward form to offend the eye. The tremendous hill upon whose eastern side Butte lays, is almost hollow with innumerable mining shafts running down vertically into the earth's crust for over half a mile, and horizontal levels that cross them at every 100 feet. Near its top scores of great derricks are clustered close together, and always near at hand one sees the buildings that house the powerful engines that pull 20 tons of ore up the deep shaft at a surprising speed. Other houses, where electric engines compress and store the air that operate the rock drills and keep the miners alive far down in the bowels of the earth, are close by, and add nothing to the attractiveness of the city.

From the top of the hill, which is banded by many rails for the trains which carry the ore off to the smelters (most of them being in Great Falls, Mont.), a wonderful view can be had of the main ridge of the Rockies just to the east of the city. As the top of this hill is over 6,000 feet high, the 10,000-foot elevation of the Rockies is not impressive—except to a sensitive carburetter like mine, which had to be repeatedly adjusted before it would furnish the right gas to take me up even the 6,000-foot hill. In the valley intervening between the city and the mountains, little home settlements were laid out in the clear air like the squares of a checker board, while to the south the lofty iron chimney of a great smelter belched thick clouds of green smoke.

Visiting this smelter the next afternoon, we first inspected the "concentrator" house, where the ore from the mines is crushed and sieved, then followed it to the blast furnace to see it mixed with coke and lime and melted into molten streams that run out into fire-brick carriers and are rolled to the crucible. In this retort it is again melted and clarified, and then poured out into an incandescent stream into ten-pound moulds. After these moulds of 98 per cent. pure copper are cooled, they are shipped to refineries in the East.

Labor Unions in Absolute Control.

That evening the manager of the Montana Henderson agency took us out to the "Gardens," Butte's only green spot and playground, located in a little gulch in the lower slopes of the Rockies; and later on a tour of Butte's unique tenderloin. As the mines are run night and day by three shifts of eight-hour-day men (mostly Slavs and Hungarians), the streets of Butte are usually crowded with the "shifts" that are off duty. The men having no other amusement than intoxication, the saloons are as thick as telephone poles, and drunkenness so common as to attract no attention.

Before leaving for the East we had a personal demonstration of the power of the local unions, in our garage. Wishing to have a slight leak in his gasoline tank repaired, Bob had started to remove the tank when one of the mechanics came up and asked him if he had a union card. Learning that Bob was not a registered mechanic, he called to the shop manager, who informed us that we could not work on our machines ourselves, but that we would have to hire a man to do it. Our explanation that we wanted him to solder the leak, but that we did not propose to pay him a dollar an hour for the part of the work we could do ourselves, had no effect. In the end we had to take the machine out of the garage, remove the tank on the sidewalk; when for spite we took it to another place to be fixed.

A union plumber in Butte was recently fined $50 for stopping a leak in the water piping of his own house one night, because the rules required that he call in another plumber. But if he had done so, the other plumber would not have come, being forbidden to work after hours. In spite of its limitations, however, the native sons are very loyal to Butte and are good boosters.

Leaving Butte for the Rockies, late one afternoon, bedecked with the few of our original pennants that had not been stolen, and burdened with no regrets at our departure, although escorted to the "Five Mile House" by two local enthusiasts, we soon passed the city race track, gay with the height of the season, and entered a long canyon decorated with occasional picnic parties. At the foot of the "18-mile hill" (two miles long, 18 miles from Butte), I stopped to put on my low-gear sprocket, and succeeded in gaining the top of the long grade leading to the summit of the Continental Divide, with little trouble. Bob, however, could not get his carburetter right, so I had a full hour to enjoy the panorama of surrounding peaks stretching to the north and south, before he arrived (for now the road had attained an altitude of 6,230 feet, and I was in the heart of the Rockies—on the rest of the Continental Divide's lowest pass).

Another Night of Sleepless Torment.

"It'll be all down hill the rest of the way," I said to Bob, by way of encouragement; but I was all wrong, as we found out later. Starting down the first decline I had met since leaving the Bitter Roots, we soon caught up with a tiny stream flowing east, and wondered to think that it could find a down grade upon which to flow through its thousands of miles of travel clear to the Gulf of Mexico. The realization that this was possible—to flow for 4,000 miles steadily down hill, made us feel that we had gotten pretty high up in the world.

TYPICAL PROSPECTOR'S SHACK IN MONTANA WILDERNESS.

The roads through the mountainous plateau that now stretched on ahead were soft and sandy and rough in spots; but neither the roads nor the grades anywhere in the Rockies offer the obstacles that we met continually in the Bitter Roots. Supping at Whitehall, the first settlement east of Butte, about 8 PM, we continued a few miles farther and then lay down beside our machines to spend the most miserable night of our lives. While the moon was magnificent, the cold not intense, and the ground not unbearably hard, the mosquitoes which swarmed about us so thickly that the air literally hummed with the noise of their wings, tortured us so incessantly that we couldn't get a minute's sleep. As it grew colder towards morning and the ground became harder and harder, we took turns getting up and venting our rage by switching the empty air violently. But the pests abated none of their bloodthirsty vigor, and in the early morning light (when it came at last) seemed more husky then ever.

*A STRETCH OF GOOD ROAD BETWEEN
MISSOULA AND BUTTE.*

Clancy "Discovered" in Montana Wilds.

Naming our night's stopping place "Mosquito Camp No. 2," we made a quick getaway and soon were climbing again around the south base of a great mountain which the railroad passed to the north—having to cover 30 miles to the railroad's 14. The narrow, little-used roads were awful in places, frequently shaking us to jelly. Following the Northern Pacific as closely as possible, we avoided Pony and Sappington and struck the railroad again at Willow Creek, a barren, cross roads town. Here we got some green bananas and dried apricots for our breakfast, and some gas at 40 cents a gallon.

Six miles of good road now took us on to Three Forks, where we stopped an hour for Bob to repair his speedometer-cable and for me to get some cookies and a milk-shake. Twelve miles of fair roads interspersed with two of bad, led us to Logan; and 24 more miles of climbing over another lofty divide to Bozeman, a smart Western community and market center for cattle and grain. Here we caught up with a one-cylinder artist who was making his way from Anaconda, Mont., to Chicago, occasionally stopping to work at harvesting en route to pay expenses. The lad was a regular reader of Bicycling World and Motorcycle Review, and asked me if I had read about the bold youth who was touring the world on a Henderson. When I remarked that I hadn't, he seemed much disgusted and then started in to tell me all about my own adventures. Bob promptly spoiled it all, however, by giving my identity away. Not being able to hold to our pace, the lad did not accompany us, as he had desired, and soon we were climbing alone the third divide of the Rockies, on the road to Livingston. On the other side a 10-mile stretch of good road down an abandoned railroad enabled us to make up a little time and to reach Livingston in time to read a bunch of mail from home, to get some supper, and start off for Gardiner and Yellowstone Park—our next stopping place, 60 miles south—at 5 PM

Had we known what we were getting into, we could not have been hired to ride our machines up that canyon to Gardiner, nor would we have done it had we not expected to be permitted to take our machines into the Park (a Butte paper having only recently reported that the Park was now open to motor vehicles), but even the garage men told us the roads were fine and that we would have no trouble in reaching Gardiner in three hours.

Reminded of a Night in Africa.

As a matter of fact the "fine" roads were rocky and washed out and good only in spots, and the ever-increasing altitude (for Yellowstone Park is from 8,000 to 10,000 feet in the air) made some of the grades very stiff and put our mixture on the burn again. Bob got his adjustment better than I could mine this time, and at 10 PM, when I got stuck at the foot of a long, lonesome hill, I hadn't seen him for an hour. Getting out my pocket flashlight, I walked to the top of the hill, hoping that he might be waiting for me there, or that I could see a light of some habitation, but as neither greeted my eyes, I was strongly reminded of my night adventure in the mountains of Africa.

Yellowstone Park, But Barred Out.

Expecting to meet a bear or a rattlesnake or something terrible any moment, I descended to my patient machine again, tried still another adjustment on my air valve, cranked her up once again and finally made the top a-flying. Two miles further on another light in the valley far below gladdened my heart, and soon I came upon Bob anxiously awaiting me in front of the Corwin Hot Springs Hotel. Here we were glad enough to get a room, after covering 165 miles during 16 hours in the saddle. A dip in the warm mineral spring swimming tank soon after did much to take away the ache in our bones and allow us a refreshing sleep.

Continuing on the next morning, I distinguished myself by coming over the brow of a hill too rapidly to slow up enough upon the unexpectedly sharp descent on the other side without jamming my brake and locking the rear wheel. This caused me to skid head-on into the side of the cliff, smashing my lamp, bending my handlebars badly, breaking off my starting crank, but not bruising me or the machine enough to prevent a prompt continuance of the trip. The canyon, which had been walled by gray, precipitous cliffs edged with rugged skylines, patched with snow squares of white, and tinted with lovely grays and blues, now widened to resemble a serrated plateau through which the Gardiner River, which we had been following from Livingston, now cut only a shallow valley.

Soon after 10 A. M. the great stone arch forming the northern entrance to Uncle Sam's largest and most interesting park—that of the Yellowstone—informed us of our arrival at Gardiner, Mont. Here we were shocked to learn that it would be impossible to enter our machines in the park (the Butte paper being decidedly premature in its report to the contrary), and so were forced to join a Shaw & Powell stage party leaving for the interior an hour later, and leave our machines in storage at Gardiner. The native sons told us that ours were the first motorcycles to come up to the park from Livingston, so we had some consolation at having succeeded in getting that far.

The attractions of Yellowstone Park were so ably described in an April issue of Bicycling World and Motorcycle Review that I will not mention them here.

Bumping Over the Ties Again.

Arriving at Gardiner again on the evening of the fifth day we bade the ladies farewell on the train and prepared our machines for the return trip to Livingston. The four days of rain had turned the bad-enough roads into stretches of slimy gumbo, and when morning came we found we would have to take to the railroad track if we were to get back at all. Two o'clock saw us bumping along the ties of the single track road, off for Livingston, but the spaces between the ties, except for occasional stretches, and the zinc-covered trestles made our progress slow and agonizing in the extreme. Moreover, we experienced great difficulty in getting through the cow-guards placed at every cross road, and over the rails on turnouts. After three miles Bob gave it up for the road— bad as it might be—but I hung on, bumping and shaking across the ties for two miles more before also giving in to the vibration. The road necessitated the use of chains, however, and even after I had put them on provided little better going than the railroad track, which I resumed again at the foot of a long grade.

But now the track was worse than before, and nearly shaking the machine to pieces and hammering myself to pulp, and beyond the hill, when I wanted to resume the road again, a stout fence and grass-grown field precluded the possibility. With no choice but to continue the torture, I kept on down the track—and then the frame of my saddle broke, to double my agony. Whack! Thud! Down I came solid on top bar of the machine for every one of the thousands of ties I had to cross during the mile I had to cover before I could get back into the road (through a field) again; and then I was fairly sick with the punishment thereof.

CHAPTER XXV
Clancy Ends Globe Girdling Trip

**Final Installment of "'Round the World"
Tour Which Carries the Traveler from
The "Bad Lands" of Montana to the
White Lights of New York**

At dark, after seven hours of continuous struggle, we had covered only 25 of the 60 miles we had to go, and now a touring car stuck in the mud delayed us until we found our assistance would be useless. At 9:30, still fighting gumbo and rocks, we found we still had 30 miles to go, and would have crept into a nearby barn for the remainder of the night had not the merciless ache in our empty stomachs warned us that sleep would be impossible until we had food. Both our lights were glassless and both of us were exhausted through physical strain and lack of food, but we had to continue on.

To be brief, it took us two and a half hours to cover those 30 miles, over the strange, rough, slippery roads, and many were the falls we had in the treacherous mud. Once I struck a two-foot stone head on in the darkness and was thrown eight feet before I hit the ground, to roll over and over again. Luckily, Bob was not far behind, and after turning off my prostrate motor, could care for me. Sick to my stomach from the shock of the fall, I escaped serious injury, as usual, but could not move my left arm for some minutes. Soon, however, we were off again, my wonderful Henderson being even tougher than I, and by midnight arrived in Livingston, surprised to be alive, only to find both garages locked for the night. Finally the watchman for one of them showed up and, having put our steeds to bed, raced to a restaurant and spent 70 cents each before our hunger had been satisfied.

Big Things That Interested.

We took the next day off to rest up, and were maddened the following morning to find it had rained hard all night and might not let up for a week. Towards night it cleared up a bit and revealed the Rocky Mountains to the south and north all clothed in snow, including the mountains in the park. The glimmering snow mantle made the mountains look much more like their pictures and formed an inspiring sight. To get a better view of them, we walked down by the railroad station and there discovered something even more interesting—two of the giant Mallet compound-articulated freight locomotives (double the length of the ordinary freight locomotive) which are used to push the rear half of trains up the long grade of the divide we had come over between Bozeman and Livingston. Being such huge brutes—the largest locomotives in the world—I longed to ride on one.

ONE OF MONTANA'S MANY ROCKY RIVERS.

A Ride Up Hill in Locomotive Cab.

Before long the tiny engineer of "4002," later known as "Bill," came around to inspect the monster, and I plied him with questions concerning his steed. In the course of our conversation he discovered that we were the two youths that he had read about in his paper that morning, so I did not have much trouble in coaxing him to let us ride up to the top of the Divide and back with him that night. Finally, having pledged us to absolute secrecy, he told us to climb on at a switch half a mile above the town, where he would pass at 9 o'clock that night. We got some cigars for him, and at 9 o'clock were excitedly waiting "at the switch." Soon the arc-light of the "road" locomotive at the head of the train that had just come in from the East was turned on, and then it came labouring up the track followed by a long "string" of cars. It took several minutes for the train to pass us, while we were experiencing many of the sensations of the brake-beam hobo and the train robber intermingled, and then at the end, shoving behind and showering sparks, came our fiery chariot "4002" in full action.

Just beyond the switch the train slowed up for a minute and we clambered aboard the mammoth engine to be welcomed by both the engineer and the fireman, who were soon enjoying our cigars. At once the throbbing engine was at work again, the little engineer tugging at one mysterious lever, pushing another, turning out one valve and shutting a second, while the fireman almost constantly shovelled coal into the white-hot maw of the giant fire-box to keep the steam pressure constant at 200 pounds. Slowly the heavy train kept plugging up the mountain's side, but the rain and darkness were so thick I could see only a glimmer where the road locomotive was straining away ahead, and nothing but a green light behind. Occasionally a vivid lightning flash lit up the whole sky, accompanied by thunder.

Nearly Suffocated in a Tunnel.

Soon we could discern snow in the ditch beside the track and when we held out our arms found the rain had turned to snow in the higher altitude. Now a short tunnel nearly smothered us with sulphurous smoke and gave impressive warning of the three-quarter mile tunnel ahead. When we neared it the engineer told us to bunch up our handkerchiefs and hold them tight over our nose and mouth, as he did, and with doors and windows shut tight in the cab, we entered the long, smoke-filled hole. The following seven minutes came the nearest thing to being hell that I ever hope to experience. The smoke, or sulphurous gas and smoke, oozed into the cab from a hundred cracks, and as the firebox promptly burned up most of the available oxygen while the heat became more and more intense, we were soon being suffocated in three different ways at once. It was just like sucking the fumes of a sulphur match and nothing else into your lungs. Every breath was torture, yet we all had to breathe very fast to get enough oxygen to keep alive. The helplessness of it all was anguish, too, for we could not have then bettered our condition had we had a mountain of gold—and the fireman had just told us of a predecessor of his who had been asphyxiated in that same tunnel the summer before. At the time I could imagine no worse death than smothering in such gripping gas.

Luckily the tunnel was no longer, and then—my! How good that fresh air tasted! The lead mine had been paradise compared with that tunnel. But now we had been detached from the train we had helped up the grade, and after a talk with the lonely section signal man, started back the grade, so did not mind either tunnel. Leaning out of the window, I watched the searchlight at the front illumine the track for miles ahead until we were secretly dropped off again at a crossing just above the station. The great engine had shaken and jarred so badly coming down that we had to fill up with a midnight supper before hitting the hay.

"MOSQUITO CAMP" BESIDE CLARK'S FORK RIVER, MONTANA.

Over Eastern Montana's "Bad Lands."

Rain and mud imprisoned us in Livingston two days longer, but at last we got away for the East and kept the Rockies in sight until we had gone 50 miles. There were few grades, but the half-dried gumbo was awful. At the smart city of Billings we joined the flat, muddy stream of the Yellowstone and continued along beside it through the lustreless settlements and towns of Custer, Sanders, Forsyth, and Roseburg to Niles City, and then to Glendive, where it turned north. Our route also paralleled that of the Northern Pacific Railroad, which we followed clear to Bismarck and across North Dakota, for that matter. Near Glendive (eastern Montana) we encountered the bad lands, a great stretch of useless country that looked as if it had never been finished, or else an original table land had been worn away except in spots by the action of water, wind and erosion, leaving the present formations to suggest castles, esquimaux huts, dagobas, gorges in miniature, earthquake crevasses, domes, and everything crazy in strata. Here the hills came down grade sharp to a dead level without any curve at the bottom, and often rose as abruptly again. Deep sand and few bridges also delayed our passage through this God-forsaken district.

Through Prosperous North Dakota.

North Dakota, on the other hand, proved to be an ideal State for motoring, at least in the dry season, which we had now entered. Almost as soon as we crossed the border line we noticed the great difference between it and Montana agriculturally, also. Now spreading grain fields extended on both sides of us, and every little town sported its elevator and at least one bank. The absence of "saloon" signs to stare us in the face was so marked that we made inquiries as to the cause thereof and learned that

North Dakota was a "dry" State. If the apparent prosperity of the State, evident on all sides, had in any way resulted from this constitutional prohibition law, we felt that it would be a splendid idea for Montana to follow her sister State's example. The five-year old town of Beach, even, had five banks.

When we reached Bismark, the capital of North Dakota, we were surprised to find it a city of only 10,000 inhabitants. Continuing straight across the center of the State over excellent black-dirt roads, and through endless prairies smiling with waving fields of grain, we came to Jamestown and later to Fargo, the largest city in the State, and yet with a population of only 30,000.

In Minnesota, the country changed gradually from flat to rolling; trees, woods and lakes began to appear. Heading southwest for Minneapolis, and striking much sand near Little Falls, we rode through miles and miles of corn and grain fields. Allen ahead, around a bend, seemed to be riding right through the field itself, and often the road formed the dividing line between a sea of wheat to the north and an ocean of corn to the south. Yet there was plenty of land in central Minnesota uncultivated.

Minneapolis disappointed us in not being so live and modern as we had expected, and we saw surprisingly few motorcycles there. We laid over a day here to rest up and view the falls of Minnehaha and the University of Minnesota buildings, and began to enjoy Eastern prices again—15 cents for three eggs instead of 35 cents.

Chicago But No "Great White Way."

On our way to St. Paul, 10 miles east, we passed Edward Payson Weston finishing the last lap of his long hike from New York; and it comforted me to think that at last I was at least within walking distance of home. In St. Paul our route took us directly past the beautiful capital building of Minnesota, but its splendor was not at all typical of the business buildings that lined the narrow streets of St. Paul's commercial center.

Just east of Minneapolis we had crossed the muddy Mississippi, and soon after leaving St. Paul we entered Wisconsin on good, hard (with a tendency toward sandiness), level roads. Steering for Madison, we passed through Eau Claire, surrounded by fields of wheat already stacked by power harvesters, skirted the edge of many small, prosperous farms, including their individual corn patch and other welcome reminders of the East; and here encountered some hills worthy of the name again. In Madison, a beautiful city of lakes, we saw another State capitol, a new one in process of construction, this time; and then turned south to make a week's visit to my brother's home in the college town of Beloit. One of the city's newspapers here honored me with a three-column head to the front page story of my trip.

The roads of Illinois were not so good as those of Wisconsin, on account of sand and heavy traffic, and the signposts were most inconsistent in stating mileage to Chicago. When I left Rockford the distance read 88.8 miles, and after I had covered the 14 miles to Belvidere I found I still had 84 to go. Near Elgin I struck a four-mile stretch of its almost perfect race-track, and held the throttle wide open to my heart's content. Between Elgin and Chicago the roads were in terrible condition. Twenty miles out of Chicago, in the fast-gathering darkness, I crashed suddenly into an unseen hole and my rear wheel's rim bent in with a crunch. Inspection revealed only three spokes broken, however, so I continued slowly on and caught up with two twin riders who were stuck with a puncture. After helping them to repair it and hearing in silent amusement all about their exciting adventures upon their tremendous 200-mile tour upstate, they guided me into the city to the Henderson factory branch on Michigan avenue.

Here the boys received me most cordially, entertained me at their homes, and the next two days rode me all over the city in a sidecar, while my service-scarred machine was exhibited in the show window. I was agreeably impressed with the extensive park system of the city which provides 40 miles of boulevards for local motorists, and spent a very enjoyable evening at the Chicago Motorcycle Club's comfortable home; but I couldn't find any "Great White Way" in Chicago, nor many of the individual characteristics that make New York the greatest city in the world.

The End of the Long Trip.

As Allen wished to visit some friends in Chicago, I continued east all alone, except for my escort which Mr. Davis of the Henderson branch formed as far as South Bend, Ind. At Toledo I turned north to make my return visit at the Henderson factory in Detroit, and here received a warm welcome, while my steed, which had certainly done itself proud, was looked up to in mute admiration by its many young brothers who had appeared upon the scene during its long and brilliant absence from home.

The remainder of the tour through Cleveland (where I regretted lack of time to accept the invitation of the Goodyear Tire & Rubber Co. to visit its plant in Akron, 20 miles south), Reading, Buffalo, and Syracuse to Albany was devoid of any special incident. But in Western New York I found the best long stretches of road of anywhere in the world. Not being able to resist the temptation of surprising the folks in their summer home before ending at New York, I entered Massachusetts east of Albany and spent one night with the family in the Berkshire

Hills, which acquired new beauty when seen through my now "Continentalized" vision.

Connecticut, a corner of which I passed through on my final run to New York, made the 16th State I had ridden in since leaving San Francisco—over 5,000 miles somewhere back.

A moving picture camera photographed my triumphal entrance into Manhattan, and marked the end of my 11 months' journey.

EPILOGUE
Around the World on a Henderson

(Published in the September 4, 1914, issue
of *Motorcycle Illustrated Magazine*)

CARL STEARNS CLANCY, the New York newspaper man, who left the Metropolis last October, returned to this city August 27. During the last ten months Mr. Clancy's 1912 Henderson motorcycle has carried him over 18,000 miles, through Ireland, Scotland, England, Holland, Belgium, France, Spain, Algiers and Tunis, Africa, Italy, India, Federated Malay States, China, Japan, and on a most strenuous transcontinental trip from San Francisco east, via Portland, Ore.; Spokane, Wash.; Wallace, Idaho; Butte, Mont.; Yellowstone Park, Bismarck, N. D.; Minneapolis and Chicago.

After visiting the Henderson factory in Detroit Mr. Clancy started on the last leg of his tour for New York.

Establishing Henderson Agencies

ONE of the interesting points in connection with this first girdle of the globe by motorcycle is the fact that Mr. Clancy has been working his way by establishing foreign sales agencies for the Henderson, and by writing magazine articles while en route. He has travelled in the most inexpensive way, and camped out often at night, and experienced many narrow escapes. Between Paris and San Francisco Mr. Clancy travelled entirely alone, but from California east he has been accompanied by Mr. Robert Allen, of Los Angeles, who is riding a 1913 Henderson.

Mr. Clancy states that the road conditions in the United States are far worse than in any other country, having been held down to as low as 20 miles during a 14-day struggle.

"I found the worst roads of all in northern California, eastern Idaho and western Montana. During one two-hour stretch I had seventeen falls on account of loose rocks and mud. The Bitter Root Mountains proved a much greater obstacle than the Rockies," he continued. "The most remarkable feature of the whole trip is the surprising endurance of my machine, which now seems to be running as well as ever, in spite of the 18,000 miles it has in its bones."

Lessons of the Long Tour

"WHILE I have thoroughly enjoyed my trip and profited by every mile of it," continued the globe-circler, "I must say that the motorcyclist who undertakes such a tour should carefully consider all the risks entailed. The up-to-date motorcycle is just about as dependable a piece of mechanism as a chap would care to handle, but it must be remembered that there are some geographical conditions beyond the prowess of even the sturdiest single-tracker. Routes should be mapped with the utmost care, and plenty of time should be given to collecting data relative to general traveling conditions in the various countries to be entered, so that the tourist may not find himself hemmed in by precipitous mountains or some other barrier and forced to make a hundred-mile detour. Such conditions may easily be encountered on a 'round-the-world tour by motorcycle, and only constant watchfulness can keep the rider out of trouble.

"It is a great consolation, however, to know that one's mount is going to be equal to all kinds of rough going and that the danger of a mishap between towns that may be fifty miles apart is reduced to the minimum. The tourist who undertakes such a long jump with the limited baggage and tools which can be carried over a rough country is bound to take a few chances, but if his mount is worthy of his confidence he will get through and be all the more an enthusiast for his experience. The unusual happenings along my route would make quite a book, but they cannot be dealt with in a brief statement. Suffice it to say that there were thrills enough to meet my requirements at all times.

The Value of a Partner

"I MAY say in passing that a party of two or three riders can derive much more enjoyment from a world tour than a single rider. I was accompanied throughout much of the journey, of course, but I was also called upon to make some long and trying jumps alone. These experiences convinced me that much of the fascination of the motorcycle lies in the spirit of companionship that it encourages. There is so much to be seen and discussed along even the most ordinary foreign route that the rider who travels alone soon finds that he is missing something. He needs a congenial partner.

"American riders are already pretty well posted on touring conditions in eastern European countries, but they know little or nothing of riding conditions in the Far East for the very simple reason that in practically all of this territory the motorcycle is a newcomer.

The Educational Value

"IT WOULD be difficult to overestimate the educational value of such a tour as I have just completed, for I feel safe in saying that by no other means could I have obtained the broad insight into conditions in foreign countries that has resulted from my motorcycle journey. In many countries I reached districts inaccessible to the automobile and far from lines of ordinary travel and thus was brought into touch with the great rank and file of the people. In the cities certain allowances are made for tourists, and the traveler who wishers to obtain a true knowledge of living conditions must go where he is not expected. This is what I tried to do throughout my entire trip and the results have been sufficiently interesting to justify the additional trouble sometimes involved.

"I do not know that I will ever make another 'round-the-world trip, but if I do it may be depended upon that I will travel by motorcycle and that my mount will be as nearly a duplicate of the Henderson I now have as possible. I do not see how any machine could have behaved more satisfactorily under the widely varying conditions to which it was subjected."

ABOUT THE AUTHOR

Professional motorcycle adventurer Dr. Gregory W. Frazier is the only motorcyclist known to have five times circumnavigated the globe by motorcycle. He has been described as "America's #1 extreme motorcycle adventurer." No stranger to danger, his adventures around the earth include having been shot at by rebels, jailed by unfriendly authorities, bitten by snakes, run over by Pamplona bulls and smitten by a product of Adam's rib.

Frazier's two-wheel travels have taken him over 1,000,000 miles and he has literally ridden a motórcycle to the ends of the earth: Deadhorse, Alaska; Ushuaia, Argentina; North Cape, Norway; Cape Agulhas, South Africa; and Bluff, New Zealand. He continues today to actively pursue two-wheel adventures at distant places on the planet as well as in North America.

Frazier works as an author, motorcycle journalist, film producer and professional photographer. His treatments appear widely throughout the international motorcycling press. Known for his travel and adventure articles, he also enjoys a solid reputation for motorcycle and product evaluations.

Books published include:

- *Alaska by Motorcycle*
- *Europe by Motorcycle*

- *New Zealand by Motorcycle*
- *Riding South: Mexico, Central America and South America by Motorcycle*
- *Motorcycle Sex: Or Freud Would Never Understand the Relationship between Me and My Motorcycle*
- *Motocycle Poems by the Biker Poet*
- *Motorcycle Cemetery Tales*
- *Indian Motorcycle International Suppliers Directory*
- *BMW GSing Around the World*
- *Riding the World*
- *Motorcycle Touring—Everything You Need to Know*
- *On the Road—Successful Motorcycle Touring*

As a documentary film producer, Frazier made numerous contributions to the film industry and motorcycling history with films such as:

- *Vintage Iron*
- *Mexico by Motorcycle*
- *Motorcycling on the Ten Best Highways in America*
- *Motorcycling on the Ten Best Highways in the Alps*
- *Motorcycling to Alaska*
- *Roadkill*
- *Motorcycling Down Under (Australia and New Zealand)*
- *Two-Wheel Wanderlust—Traveling Around the World by Motorcycle*
- *Motorcycle Adventuring in Southeast Asia and the Orient*

Dr. Frazier is also an accomplished professional motorcycle racer, having won races with BMW and Indian motorcycles. His name can be found in the Pikes Peak Race Course record books aboard both marquees, and road race tracks throughout the United States and Canada have seen him as a successful competitor on a wide variety of race bikes, including Honda and Yamaha. As the founder of the *Big Dog Adventure Ride (www. horizonsunlimited.com/ bigdog/)* and the *Elephant Ride*, he has enjoyed both events as organizer and entrant.

Frazier is a well-known motivational speaker, oftentimes presenting his multimedia show "Sun Chasing—Five Times Around The World By Motorcycle—Ride The World."

As a global circumnavigator, he completed his fifth motorcycle ride around the earth while helping a Parkinson's patient "Ride the Dream," taking her as a passenger on the back. She had never been on a motorcycle before she met Frazier and asked him to carry her around the globe. Their trip lasted 14 months and covered nearly 30,000 miles. The Web site *www.ultimategloberide. com* follows their wild adventures as they circled the globe.

www.horizonsunlimited.com/gregfrazier is his home base on the Internet. His work on *Motorcycle Adventurer* and a supplemental CD of the original photographs, magazine articles and Henderson motorcycle sales material can be purchased from the Whole Earth Motorcycle Center *(www.motorcycleadventurer.com)*.

When not adventuring around the world, Frazier, a Crow Indian ("Sun Chaser"), lives quietly in the Big Horn Mountains of Montana on the Crow Indian Reservation. Frazier says of his personal adventures, "I hate adventure that has anything to do with snakes or sharks."